Praise for

English Lessons

"Luminous patience and insight lights these uncommonly thoughtful pages. Andrea Lucado is a winsome, wise, and unwaveringly honest companion for the wonderer and wanderer, and the lines on these pages offer a tangible lifeline to every God-wrestler. These are pages that are hard to put down, that you will want to return to and reread. Andrea not only offers a genuine way to love the questions themselves, she offers an authentic way to love the Answer Himself."

—ANN VOSKAMP, author of the *New York Times* bestsellers
The Broken Way and *One Thousand Gifts*

"This book brought me right back to a younger self—a bookish pastor's daughter living abroad, making sense of her faith, of the world and her place in it. Andrea is a lovely writer, and this story will make you ache for the feelings and memories and experiences of your early twenties—both the wonderful ones and the challenging ones. And it will make you want to go to Oxford, of course."

—SHAUNA NIEQUIST, *New York Times* best-selling author
of *Present Over Perfect* and *Bread & Wine*

"*English Lessons* is positively paradoxical—both mature and youthful, entertaining and challenging, full of light and full of depth. Written by a pastor's daughter, it is the perfect book for those trying to own a faith handed to them by someone else. Whether you're a spiritual seeker or a hardened skeptic, this book will both honor your doubts and open your heart to grace. A wonderful paradox, indeed!"

—JONATHAN MERRITT, contributing writer for *The Atlantic*
and author of *Jesus Is Better Than You Imagined*

"To have a strong faith we can stand on, we all need to wrestle well with hard questions and come face-to-face with our gut-honest feelings. Andrea does this in such a tenderly beautiful way that will leave the deep parts of your heart feeling comforted and understood."

—LYSA TERKEURST, *New York Times* best-selling author
and president of Proverbs 31 Ministries

"In *English Lessons* we discover an honest voice exploring life and love, finding that it's okay and even common to not know where the journey will take you. Andrea Lucado's memoir is a story of love and friendship, saying goodbyes, and seeing yourself in a mirror to find out more of who you really are, perhaps for the first time. Her year in Oxford was a wide-open space for a life of grace."

—SCOT MCKNIGHT, Julius R. Mantey Chair of New
Testament, Northern Seminary

"English Lessons is one of those beautiful books that you can just fall into. Andrea's story, her retelling, her insight, her heart—it all shines. I love this book, I learned from it, and I cannot wait to read it again."

—ANNIE F. DOWNS, best-selling author of *Looking for
Lovely* and *Let's All Be Brave*

"In this vivid and vulnerable memoir, Andrea Lucado allows readers to experience both the charms and the challenges of living in a foreign place. Andrea's story gives readers permission to have faith like a child, questions like a teenager, and steady trust like an adult. If you want your own faith to grow and to grow up, this well-rendered story is for you."

—KATELYN BEATY, editor at large, *Christianity Today*,
and author of *A Woman's Place*

English
Lessons

English Lessons

THE CROOKED PATH OF
GROWING TOWARD FAITH

Andrea Lucado

WATERBROOK

English Lessons

All Scripture quotations are taken from the Holy Bible, New International Version®, NIV®. Copyright © 1973, 1978, 1984 by Biblica Inc.® Used by permission. All rights reserved worldwide. Scripture quotations marked (ESV) are taken from the ESV® Bible (the Holy Bible, English Standard Version®), copyright © 2001 by Crossway, a publishing ministry of Good News Publishers. Used by permission. All rights reserved.

Details in some anecdotes and stories have been changed to protect the identities of the persons involved.

Hardcover ISBN 978-1-60142-895-0
eBook ISBN 978-1-60142-896-7

Published in the United States by WaterBrook, an imprint of the Crown Publishing Group, a division of Penguin Random House LLC, New York.

WATERBROOK® and its deer colophon are registered trademarks of Penguin Random House LLC.

Library of Congress Cataloging-in-Publication Data
Names: Lucado, Andrea, author.
Title: English lessons : the crooked path of growing toward faith / Andrea Lucado.
Description: First Edition. | Colorado Springs, Colorado : WaterBrook, 2017.
Identifiers: LCCN 2016053341 (print) | LCCN 2017010225 (ebook) | ISBN 9781601428950 (hardcover) | ISBN 9781601428967 (electronic)
Subjects: LCSH: Lucado, Andrea. | College students—Religious life. | Oxford Brookes University.
Classification: LCC BV4531.3 L78 2017 (print) | LCC BV4531.3 (ebook) | DDC 248.8/34—dc23
LC record available at https://lccn.loc.gov/2016053341

Printed in the United States of America
2017—First Edition

10 9 8 7 6 5 4 3 2 1

For my parents, and always for my parents

Contents

English Lesson   xi

1. Field Crickets   1

2. The Babel Effect   15

3. My Front Light   33

4. The Atheist Society   57

5. The Faith of Our Fathers   69

6. A Spoon in My Tea   79

7. The Road More Traveled   95

8. If I Forget You, O Jerusalem   113

9. English Gardens   131

10. River Conversations   149

11. The 0.1-Mile Pilgrimage   159

12. Pillars   177

13. Good-Byes at Kazbar   199

14. Tumbleweeds   213

Acknowledgments   223

English Lesson

Life cannot be understood flat on a page. It has to be lived; a person has to get out of his head, has to fall in love, has to memorize poems, has to jump off bridges into rivers, has to stand in an empty desert and whisper sonnets under his breath:

> I'll tell you how the sun rose,
> A ribbon at a time . . . [1]

And so my prayer is that your story will have involved some leaving and some coming home, some summer and some winter, some roses blooming out like children in a play. My hope is your story will be about changing, about getting something beautiful born inside of you, about learning to love a woman or a man, about learning to love a child, about moving yourself around water, around mountains, around friends, about learning to love others more than we love ourselves, about learning oneness as a way of understanding God. We get

---

1. Emily Dickinson, *The Complete Poems of Emily Dickinson*, Part 2, Nature.

one story, you and I, and one story alone. God has established the elements, the setting and the climax and the resolution. It would be a crime not to venture out, wouldn't it?

It might be time for you to go. It might be time to change, to shine out.

I want to repeat one word for you:

Leave.

Roll the word around on your tongue for a bit. It is a beautiful word, isn't it? So strong and forceful, the way you have always wanted to be. And you will not be alone. You have never been alone. Don't worry. Everything will still be here when you get back. It is you who will have changed.

—Donald Miller, *Through Painted Deserts*

I

Field Crickets

Church was not a part of my childhood. It was my childhood. Church, growing up—they twine themselves in my memories. They are the same color, indistinguishable. From my younger years, I remember more about the building itself than the words said within it. I remember the pews were classic, sturdy ones with rough blue cushions that fit nicely and would give you carpet burn if you crawled along them for too long. I remember the communion table from a vantage point underneath it, looking through the wooden slats and holding on to them, demanding my friends "let me out of jail." I remember where the communion grape juice and yeast-free crackers were stored, in the closet to the right of the stage in the auditorium. Sometimes we shoveled the crackers into our mouths while our parents had postchurch, prelunch conversations with fellow church members for what felt like forever.

Many Sundays, when I finished stealing the communion crackers, I was off to find my mom so I could tug at her, pull her arm in the direction of the door, and make it perfectly clear I was ready to leave. She was so good at not budging, standing her ground and remaining in conversation with whomever it was, as if a child were not yelling, "Mom! Mom! Mooom!" over and over at her side.

The church was built in the 1950s. Not beautiful, in a strange octagonal shape on a road called Fredericksburg. Home is what it felt like most of the time. So many people knew my name there. I didn't know their names, but I wasn't expected to. They heard my dad talk about me from the pulpit each week. I never heard their dads talk about them. Their faces were enough for me. Synonymous with the building itself. For me so many members existed only inside that building, as if they emerged from the walls on Sunday mornings and melted back into them afterward.

My neighborhood streets were the back hallways and classrooms of that octagonal-shaped building. My neighborhood friends were the daughters of elders and staff members. We got to know each other lingering outside our fathers' offices, playing hide-and-seek. We did church-league basketball together and popped gum during Sunday school together. When we reached the sixth grade, we decided, together, that we had outgrown the church playground and developed the habit of forming circles to talk and gossip with our arms crossed, our weight on one foot, hips out to one side.

Church determined my social life as well as my weekly calendar. Sunday mornings were busy; therefore, Saturday night was early curfew night, a rule I openly hated and disagreed with until the day I left home for college. Sunday nights were for small-group gatherings called life groups. Wednesdays were for midweek service. Spring break was the youth ski trip to Colorado. Christmas was always spent at home because of Christmas Eve service. Summer was for church camp. This is what I knew. This is what deep down, beneath my teenage angst and complaining, I loved. I grew up in church and church grew down into me, as if my body housed a tree of church lessons whose limbs grew inside me and rooted my feet into the church's ground itself.

This is why when people talk about how wonderful their childhood church experience was, or how terrible it was, it's difficult for me to understand why they don't simply say growing up was wonderful or growing up was terrible. How are those two things not twined for them like they are for me?

When your father has been a pastor at the same church in the same city for three decades, people come to recognize your family. At school, everyone knew I was a preacher's daughter. At church, I was Max's, the pastor's daughter.

For some, faith and belief are learned over time, understood and accepted. For those like me, faith and belief have been written into your name. Your family's profession is, in a way, Christianity. It makes "owning one's faith" an impossible and confusing feat. For how could I own my last name more than I already do?

Considering my background, you can imagine how I relate to someone with a completely unchurched childhood. That person might as well be from a tiny island off the coast of nowhere near the edge of the universe. This is why when I found myself one day in the early fall of 2008 sitting in a classroom surrounded by tiny islands off the coasts of nowhere near the edge of the universe, I marveled. Nothing about us, our pasts, or our backgrounds braided together. We were from different countries and different continents with the common goal of achieving master's degrees in English Literature. Now we have all returned to our respective origins, but then we had landed mere blocks from each other in a city called Oxford in a country called England.

Oxford. The place that makes you want to write books about it. It sucks in students from various nations on this earth, plops them together into graduating classes, and then either promptly shuttles them back home or loses them in its dark office corridors forever. I got out. Though it would have been magical to stay.

It was orientation day at Oxford Brookes University when I first met them all, the tiny islands. I left my parents waving at the bottom of a hill as I climbed up toward campus. Mom and Dad had flown over with me to help with the transition, and walking away from them that afternoon felt harder than it should have for a twenty-two-year-old. I left too early, worried I would be late, so I walked slowly as I neared the building.

I had been to Oxford before. As a junior in college, I participated in a study-abroad program there. My three best friends and I made the journey from Abilene Christian University in West Texas all the way to England to spend four months living with fellow American students and traveling on the weekends. We clutched our Rick Steves guides and felt very grown up as we sat in pubs at the ripe, legal age of twenty. We drank espresso and red wine during a memorable weeklong trip to Italy. We learned how to buy train tickets and book hostels, and we often huddled together on our bunk beds and listed the things from home we longed for: our cars, Mexican food, big grocery stores, Sonic. When we landed at the Dallas/Fort Worth International Airport in December, we felt relief and triumph. We had survived a semester overseas. And I vowed quietly to myself that one day I would return.

I don't think two more opposite cities exist, Oxford and Abilene. One is in the Cotswolds, known for endless waves of countryside at the cost of endless waves of rain. The other is in the part of Texas known for tumbleweeds, oil, more wind and dust than rain, and, of course, the occasional dreaded cricket infestation.

I call it The Summer of the Crickets, and I can still feel its heat. Thick, consuming heat that settled and lingered over Abilene adamantly for three months. I had stayed in Abilene for my last summer before my senior year. I took summer school in the morning and worked in the afternoon, and then at night, when it was finally safe to go outside without absolutely melting, I would run around campus. Even though the sun had been down for hours, I still dripped all the way. Hot and humid—the ideal environment for cricket reproduction. Every few years Abilene and other regions in Texas are overrun by crickets that hatch in warm, moist environments. That summer they took over. In the building where my summer class met, an entire wall fell victim to crickets. Thousands of them spread out among the bricks, claimed their space, and held on until fall. I don't think they moved for months. Each morning the wall of crickets remained. Class was canceled a couple of times due to the smell. Decaying crickets, I learned, have a distinct smell, similar to the aroma of stale Mexican-food leftovers with a little fresh fertilizer mixed in. Pleasant. Intoxicating.

One morning I showed up at my Latin American Authors class to find that my professor, who was also a decent artist, had drawn a picture on the whiteboard of a giant cricket with bulging red eyes and a gas mask. The picture remained on the whiteboard for weeks. I stared at it each day while he lectured. I hated those crickets. They left us alone in the classrooms, but the moment we entered the hallway, they hurled their bodies from one wall to the opposite one, creating an obstacle course between us and the exit. To make it from one building to the next was to run a cricket gantlet. I rarely made it through without getting hit. I think hell might be an eternal summer of crickets living, multiplying, and dying. There is nothing worse than your world being overrun by an insect you can't control. Kill one, turn around, and there are thirty others. You have no choice but to coexist with them until the cooler weather kills them off.

I've since learned that this particular cricket infestation was one of the worst Abilene had seen in years. The crickets we were stepping on and running away from are known as field crickets. This name sounds inaccurate to me. I think they should be called "field, road, building, bathroom, inside-your-own-freaking-car crickets." But I'm not the expert here. I started to do more research in order to understand this species better and why they came out with such a vengeance that summer in West Texas, but I decided the creatures that ruined my life those few months were not worth the time and effort to be fully understood. I don't care about their biological origins, and I certainly don't care about their benefits to our ecosystem. So my cricket knowledge is limited. I do know they can lay up to four hundred eggs at once—a fact that both terrifies and annoys me—and I know they shed their skin up to nine times before becoming adult crickets. The process of shedding skin is called "molting"—an appropriately gross-sounding word, I think. *Moooolllllting.* It takes about six weeks for the molting process to be complete and the cricket to reach full-fledged adulthood. Then they mate and lay trillions of eggs. Then, they die. Well, some live for three or four more weeks enjoying their molted state, but most of them die.

One lifetime, nine layers.

I should probably explain that Oxford Brookes University is a separate university from the one I like to call *Oxford* Oxford. It is more recently established—though I suppose everything is more recently established than a university where teachers were already teaching in AD 1096—and it uses lecture-style teaching rather than the intimate tutorial style used at *Oxford* Oxford. To distinguish between the two, most refer to Oxford Brookes as simply Brookes. Heaven forbid I should claim to be an *Oxford* Oxford student, when really I was just a normal old Brookes student. The Brookes campus is mostly concentrated in one place, on top of Headington Hill. Headington Hill boasts a city view I rarely saw. My classes were at night, so the view I remember best is distant blurs of lights, spires, and fields asleep in the dark. The daylight hours revealed lush mounds of grass playing leapfrog down the hill, a hill that was always damp from rain. Sitting at the bottom was the city center of Oxford—a dignified gathering of sixteenth-century buildings. Lined up and standing so close together, they formed one brilliant, cream-colored stone mass. Strong and old.

As I neared the building where I had been instructed to go for orientation, I felt like I might throw up. I had no idea what I was doing. I had no idea where I was going. Everything in me wanted to run all the way back down that hill into my dad's arms and ask my mom if we could go home. But I had kept my vow to return to Oxford. I had applied and been accepted. It would be silly to go back now. So I pushed through the doors, held my breath, and hoped for the best.

·☙·

I searched the room for a friendly face. There were a couple of guys standing by a table of snacks and a few people in the corner who looked like professors discussing an important piece of paper. And then I saw one. She was sitting down. She looked about my age and like someone I would have been friends with back home, and the seats beside her were empty. I made a beeline in her direction and sat down in the chair to her right.

"Hi," I said, feeling dry mouth coming on. "I'm Andrea."

"I'm Sophie," she said.

"Nice to meet you."

Sophie nodded.

"Are you from here?" I asked.

"No, no. I'm from South Africa."

"Really? That's so cool."

Sophie laughed. "Where are you from?"

"America. I mean, the States. I mean, Texas. Have you heard of Texas?"

Sophie laughed again. "Yes, I've heard of it." George W. Bush had been president for the last eight years. Of course she had heard of Texas.

Someone called for everybody to take their seats. After the program director made some introductions, we circled around the room saying our name and country of origin. I took inventory. There were about twenty of us, representing four different nations: England, India, South Africa, and the United States.

I was one of two Americans and, I would soon learn from various opinions voiced during class discussions, one of one Christian. I sat in my chair with my back straight and eyes unblinking and watched them, the tiny islands off the coasts of nowhere near the edge of the universe. So no one else in this room was like me? A pastor's daughter. A graduate of a Christian high school, where most of her friends were Christians. And now, a graduate of a Christian college, where she had only Christian friends. An employee of a Christian camp in the summers, and someone whose handful of dates were with only Christian guys. I was in a Christian sorority, the whole thing. My life to that point had been the picture of Christian-ness, and Oxford was photobombing my pretty Christian picture.

Though since birth I had spent more time inside the church walls than outside them, I had also been gifted with the ability to incessantly ask questions about my faith, which had been known to lead to periods of skepticism. My dad tells this story from when I was five years old. He was teaching me and my two sisters about the Garden of Eden. In the middle of the story, I interrupted. "Wait, if God didn't want Adam and Eve to eat from the tree, why'd he put it in the garden?" And thus my impulsively inquisitive nature reared its head. Such questions and concerns have never quite left me. I've always felt the need to ask *why?* until I get a sufficient answer.

In high school there had been a few dark and doubting months. As I recall, it started while I was outside running in our neighborhood one day. I was trying to pray, and for the first time since I had become a Christian at age nine, I felt like no one was listening to me. Instead of God's presence, I felt an emptiness, and this upset me. My logical teenage reasoning said if I couldn't feel God, he wasn't there. And if he wasn't there, I didn't have to follow his rules. And if I didn't have to follow his rules, I could do whatever I wanted. So I did, sort of, for a few months. It was a brief, slightly rebellious—by preacher's daughter standards—time in my life. And it was brought to an abrupt halt as soon as I got caught.

One of my slightly rebellious activities was sneaking out of the house. I thought sneaking out was so fun and exhilarating and, well, sneaky. One night while spending the night at my friend Leslie's, we decided, in our wisdom and maturity, to sneak out of her house and go meet up with some boys who were smoking pot. Everything went well, as it usually did. Nobody heard us leave. Nobody heard us come in. We were pros, and the night was a success. The next morning, however, was not.

A few hours after I returned home from Leslie's, I got a phone call. It was from Leslie's mom. Leslie had been overcome by a wave of guilt about what we had done the night before and told her mom everything. Now, Leslie's mom told me, either I could tell my mom or she would have to. Understandable, since Leslie's mom and my mom were good friends.

At the time, neither my mom nor my dad knew I had been doing things like sneaking out of the house. They knew I was struggling with doubt and uncertainty, but they didn't know about the recent proclamation I had made to myself that I could now do whatever I wanted because I didn't feel God's presence anymore. After I got off the phone with Leslie's mom, and after the sickness in my stomach subsided a little, I walked into my mom's room and told her everything. I told her I had been lying to her about where I was on the weekends. I told her I had snuck out of Leslie's house to hang out with boys who were smoking pot. I cried and cried and told her more details than I was planning to. She cried right along with me. She was surprised and disappointed I am sure, but I don't remember a harsh scolding or a sermon. Mostly what I remember is my mom hurting with me in an empathetic way I had not expected. And later, when my dad heard about everything, he grounded me for three weeks, but he also understood, and he also didn't yell or kick me out of the house. I saw grace in my parents that day, a grace that eventually led me back to its source.

Now in Oxford, in a class of no Christians and in a city and country that was located nowhere near the Bible Belt, I worried that I might lose the feeling of God's presence again. And if I did, how would I react this time so far away from home? Being in Oxford felt like being sixteen years old again, without the excuse of being sixteen.

As much as I hated those field crickets in Abilene that summer, I can't help but see now how like them we are, especially in those confusing years of early adulthood. The "twenties" as some call it, though I suppose this phase is not restricted to one decade. I wish our stories were more similar to the process of caterpillars turning to butterflies. That metamorphosis is such a beautiful picture, with time spent in the chrysalis (such a lovely word). But I think the reality of becoming an adult looks much more like that of a cricket nymph and its gross, painful molting process as the little runt emerges from the ground for the first time, squinting at its surroundings, struggling from one place to the other, losing skin all along the way. Probably feeling small, afraid, and lost and clinging on to building walls when it just doesn't know what else to do or where else to go.

I emerged from the ground in Oxford as a good Christian girl from the friendly state of Texas. I was twenty-two years old. I had been to college. I thought I knew things about the world and how it should be. I thought I knew about faith and God. But when I squinted my eyes at this foreign city and my new surroundings, I quickly learned that many of the things I thought I knew—about me, about faith, about others—were not necessarily true over here, in this other place, this other world. Almost as soon as I got to Oxford, I felt lost. I wandered its streets looking as cricket-nymph-like as one can possibly look. I searched for a safe wall to grab on to. A place that looked or felt like home. I looked for the God of my childhood, the faith of my childhood. But it wasn't there. I never found any rough blue pew cushions in Oxford as hard as I looked.

·⌒·

The newness and foreignness of Oxford shook me up and out and everywhere, in a way that made Oxford a scary and hard but necessary beginning for me.

Growing up, no matter when growing up happens, requires shedding layers. Especially when it comes to growing more mature in faith.

In order to learn new things, you must first unlearn old things to make space for the new things. The whole process is very sacrificial in nature, which is why it feels hard and painful and sad at any given moment. You are giving away parts of your very self, things you always held to be true. But you have to. In order to become more of the person you are, in order to believe in the God who actually is, you must get rid of the old parts that no longer make sense, revealing the truth that lies underneath. Christian Wiman wrote in his book *My Bright Abyss,* "Doubt is painful . . . but its pain is active rather than passive, purifying rather than stultifying. Far beneath it, no matter how severe its drought, how thoroughly your skepticism seems to have salted the ground of your soul, faith, durable faith, is steadily taking root."[2] I like this idea of faith lying beneath the doubt because it means that what we are looking for is within us and not outside us. When we first come out of the ground, it looks like we have a long way to travel, but really we don't have to travel to some place or arrive at some external location to find what we are looking for. We don't have to, but sometimes it does help.

---

2. Christian Wiman, *My Bright Abyss* (New York: Farrar, Straus and Giroux, 2013), 76.

2

The Babel Effect

The River Thames is England's longest river, flowing from the Cotswolds region through Oxford, then through London, and finally out to the North Sea. Some think the name *Thames* comes from the Sanskrit word *tamas,* which means "dark," because that describes the color of the water in this particular river. The Thames's waters are dark, I suppose, but compared to some opaque lakes I've spent quite a bit of time on in Texas summers, I think the color of the river is just perfect. The trees beside it are delicate and beautiful the way they watch their reflection in the surface, and the little floating boats on it look so picturesque and quiet from the bridge above. The Thames, to me, is an excellent river.

During my time in Oxford, I became very familiar with this river. More specifically, the part of the river closest to my house, where it met Donnington Bridge. A narrow path on either side was just wide enough for riding a bicycle or for two people walking while holding hands. I lived less than a mile from there, and I often found myself walking, riding, or running its muddy trail, sometimes alone, sometimes with others. The Thames provided a backdrop for many significant Oxford moments. I stared at it during the long conversation with the handsome Austrian Korean. I listened to the rain fall on it while sitting inside a cozy pub. I stood at its edge on an evening I remember clearly, when, coffee in hand, I asked God big and small questions. But before, after, and in between these events, there were runs. Many, many runs along the river when my hands got cold and my legs tired and my running shoes muddy.

The Thames was my trail that year. Just mine. It led me home and led me to strange places, conversations, and confusing feelings. A couple of times I was on the river itself in a boat, but mostly I looked at it from the edge. I watched others row on it, live on it in long, thin houseboats. It let me be an onlooker for a while, knowing I would leave in due time as most foreigners did.

A lot would happen along that river in a year, but the first would be lunch.

·⁂·

During the early weeks of my time in Oxford, I was determined to make friends at church, where all good Christians go to make friends and where all good recovering doubters go to attend their weekly meeting. I knew of a large Anglican establishment called St. Aldate's from my study-abroad semester, and I began attending immediately and faithfully each Sunday as soon as I arrived in town. Like Starbucks, church felt like my embassy in Oxford, a building in the middle of a foreign place where my membership meant something and where I felt safe and at home.

St. Aldate's met in a large, ancient building that blended in perfectly with its historic surroundings near the center of town. The inside of the church was light, with high ceilings, Roman arches, and massive stone pillars. It looked nothing like the megachurches back home, but it was, at least, a church, and there were, at least, fellow Christians all around me. The Anglican traditions of this church reminded me of my seven years spent in an Episcopalian private school in Texas. Walking forward for communion, reading liturgy, lighting candles—these old-as-the-building-itself practices lulled me into a settled and comfortable space and time, one much like when I wore a pleated skirt, kneesocks, and a necktie and sang Gregorian chants in the school choir. Except here, this time, all was done and said in the loveliest of English accents, and the staff called themselves "vicars" and "rectors."

I loved services at St. Aldate's for this reason, the way they transported me home. I did not love when service ended and I would emerge from my trance on the pew to find that the people in front of me, behind me, and to my left and right were not friendly American acquaintances but, instead, foreign English people I so desperately hoped would befriend me. Not quite tiny islands off the coasts of nowhere near the edge of the universe, but close.

Fortunately, the process of being a successful church member did not elude me like the process of cultural integration did. Inside these walls, I knew the steps to take to get involved, and I took them.

Step one: join a small group. Step two: find a place to serve or volunteer. Step three: spend time with church people outside church in order to make them your friends, in order to always have someone to eat lunch with after service. I have considered collecting these steps into some sort of pamphlet for national distribution. I would call it "Three Steps to a Successful Church Experience by Andrea Lucado (someone who has nearly thirty years of successful church experience)."

By week three in my new city, I was already in touch with a small-group leader (step one). I had signed up for worship-band tryouts (step two). I had introduced myself to members of the graduate-student group that met on Tuesday nights (step three). And by that third Sunday, I had an invitation to lunch. The steps work. Trust the steps.

I tried to hide it, but I was thrilled when my new small-group leader invited me to go out to eat with her and her husband and their friends. *This is it,* I thought. *This is the day I cross over to the English*

*side. They will be so charmed by me; they will wonder why they had
not let me into their circle sooner.*

We all cycled to the restaurant together, me and my "future
friends," as I thought of them. I clumsily trailed behind the others,
being the only one more comfortable in a car than on my bicycle. Everyone rides bikes everywhere in Oxford, and because I didn't want to
feel left out and because riding the bus was, from what I could tell,
considered not cool, an old, rusty blue bicycle had been one of my first
purchases upon moving there. The cycle to the pub took us along a
path with the river to our left and the countryside to our right. Low
fences with tiny gates protected fields with horses and cows. They
made me curious about the land inside, whose it was, and how long it
had been theirs.

Suddenly, after nothing but trail and fields for a couple of miles, a
pub appeared, and what seemed a deserted part of the river was now a
clamor of people locking up their bicycles, chatting with their friends,
and carrying shiny pints from here to there. My party chose a table in
the sun beside the water.

Although I sat near them, I felt far from my lunch companions,
my future friends. First, there was the matter of my appearance. I wore
clothes purchased from stores no one shopped in here. I had meticu-
lously straightened my hair, which, I would learn, was not exactly the
fashion for English girls. And then of course there were my teeth. I
exposed them with each nervous and uncertain smile. After some
time, I learned that having straight white teeth is not really a measure
nor standard of beauty in England. Surprisingly, the English don't see

the value of torturing their adolescents with contraptions like braces and retainers and find it odd that we Americans pay so much attention to this feature.

Besides how I looked in comparison to the others, I also struggled with the conversation. Their accents muddled things, but so did words and phrases that were familiar to me yet had new definitions in this country. Words like *fancy* and *pudding* and *pavement.* Discussing school became increasingly difficult.

"Do you have a lot of schoolwork this week?" I asked one of the guys beside me.

He laughed. "No, I haven't had any schoolwork to do for a very long time."

"Oh, your teachers must be easier than mine."

"No, it's just that here, the word *school* is used for the younger levels, which I of course haven't been in for a while."

"Oh!" I said. "Then do you have any *college* work to do?"

"No, but I do have *university* work to do," he told me.

I stared back blankly. Somehow "college" was different from "university," and neither college nor university was considered "school." This sounded needlessly complicated.

I thought life in England would be a simple transition from home. I had been there before, and, most importantly, I spoke the language. Or so I thought. In reality, no matter how similar a language seems on the page or sounds to the ear, what we actually speak is a language informed by our surroundings and upbringings. We speak our food, our weather, our societal habits and quirks. We speak what we were taught by our parents, political leaders, friends, pop-star idols, and grocery-store clerks. That's what I spoke in Oxford, and it wasn't translating well.

Lunch that day taught me a hard lesson that echoed one I had learned long before in Sunday school. It was the lesson of the Tower of Babel in Genesis, which I had conveniently forgotten until that lunch when I was forced to enter my own little tower. Remember the story?

In the beginning, "the whole world had one language and a common speech" (Genesis 11:1). Then our ancestors decided they wanted to make a name for themselves by building a tower that would reach heaven. But before they could get there, God went down to them. He said, "'Come, let us go down and confuse their language so they will not understand each other.' So the LORD scattered them from there over all the earth" (verses 7–8). It was a curse upon those trying to play God, and it was a curse I felt the consequences of that day by the river.

One of my future friends said something and everyone laughed. Everyone but me. I half smiled, trying to interpret the joke. It was no use. It was in another language I did not speak and felt I would never learn. I listened to everyone else talk for the remainder of our meal and said little myself. I watched and tried to interpret, understand, and decode the cultural scene unfolding before me, as if I were on one side of the glass and they on the other. Feeling sorry for myself and frustrated with my decision to leave a perfectly good country where things made sense to move to one where no one spoke correctly, I looked away from the table and focused on the water.

The calm river and quaint trail beside it with the sweeping branches. The abnormally perfect weather with the sun brightening different corners of our table. The beauty of it was lost in my confusion with these people I wanted, and needed, to be my friends.

Two years prior, in my study-abroad days, I had spent time on another Oxford river, the River Cherwell. Then I walked the river side by side with old friends who were American and just as in awe as I was of this city. In a spontaneous rush to do something memorable and daring on our final days in Oxford that winter, we ran from our dormitory houses toward the Cherwell wearing sweats with swimsuits underneath. All the way talking in breathless sentences about how cold the water was going to be, how the onlookers would stare at us. We didn't care. We were twenty years old and had survived a semester overseas away from our families and friends and everything familiar. We would honor the experience, cement it into our souls by jumping off a low bridge in the middle of a park near our house, into the water, in the middle of December.

I had never submerged myself in water so cold. When my body hit the river, I thought I had died. My limbs felt paralyzed. I was so consumed with the temperature I didn't know which way was up or which direction to swim. I forgot how to kick my legs or move my arms and just sort of stayed underwater for a minute, helpless. As soon as I decided I was indeed dead and had not survived the fall, my head bobbed above the surface. I heard the yells of my fellow classmates, who had not believed we would follow through, and I followed the sound of their voices to shore.

They helped pull me out, dragging me over the grassy edge as I shook, and someone covered me with a towel. Insanity pulled us into the river that day, and we smiled proudly for the cameras.

This time by the river felt different. I sat with strangers who were so polite and English and to whom the river was regular life. They didn't need to jump into it to feel some sort of rush. I walked my old, rusty bicycle home from lunch that day defeated by it all. What must they have thought of me? This American who asked so many questions about so many things and didn't laugh at their jokes.

I didn't know where the adventurous spirit was that had hurled me into the river a couple of years before. Sure, I had made it to Oxford again, but I felt so much more afraid this time and very, very alone. I watched the others from behind my side of the glass, waving and yelling for them to notice me, but when they did and finally turned to look, it was with expressions of pity.

It was not so much the lack of people as it was this cultural glass wall that created a deep sense of loneliness in me. I thought I had felt lonely before. I had felt like I had no friends before. My entire eighth-grade year, for example. But this type of loneliness was different. There was an added layer to it.

As Americans, we know that our culture is influential, so when we travel abroad, we expect to be understood by the natives. This wasn't happening at the pub. Just because we had all watched *Friends* growing up didn't mean we were alike. It was the best and worst part about living in a new country, this culturally inflicted loneliness.

A Couple of Anecdotes of Culturally Inflicted Loneliness:

- I had ridden a bike to and from class in college, but I had never navigated actual city streets on one, and I had certainly never ridden one on the other side of the road, so I was a little shaky riding a bike in Oxford at first. My first bike, the old, rusty blue one, had a basket attached to the front. I thought I looked very cute riding a bike like this, and all the other girls had baskets on their bikes too, so I felt like I fit in.

  I noticed people would put all kinds of things in their baskets: books, groceries, purses, their kids. So on my way to class one night, instead of slinging my bag over my shoulder, I placed it in my basket. It felt so nice and free to ride without any weight on my back. I was loving my basket, and I was feeling very Oxfordian and British. I saw a curb coming up ahead that I needed to hop to stay on the bike path. It wasn't a big curb; it was the flat part of the curb, raised about an inch off the ground. Flat as it was, the second I hit it, my book bag rattled in my basket, which made the basket shift left, which made my front wheel shift left, which made me shift left, all the way until I hit the ground. Before I realized what was happening, my bike, my bag, and I were scattered across the sidewalk. As I collected myself and my ego and began to stand up, I heard a group of kids yelling from across the street. At first I thought they were concerned, asking if I was okay. They weren't. They were singing in unison to the tune of nana-nana-boo-boo, "You fell off your bi-ike! You fell off your bi-ike!"

- One time I went to dinner at this guy's apartment. He and his roommates were *Oxford* Oxford people, and they had invited three other *Oxford* Oxford people and then me and one of my roommates. I would soon move in with two British girls, but at first in Oxford, I lived with two other Americans who were in town for a few months on work visas.

   The entire night was confusion. Mostly I remember one girl talking about her fiancé and how they got engaged.

   "Well, you know he is Cambridge and I'm Oxford, but he went to Eton—"

   "Where Prince William and Prince Harry went to high school?" I interjected, excited to share my knowledge of the royal family.

   "Uh, yeah," she said. "Anyways, after we had just had this dreadful fight on a train one afternoon and as we were walking off the platform, he surprised me and asked me to marry him! He gave me his Eton ring—"

"His Eton ring?" I asked.

"Yes, you know, the Eton ring. All Eton graduates have them."

I looked at my roommate. She shrugged her shoulders. Why was he giving her his class ring as an engagement ring? If he went to Cambridge, why doesn't he have some fancy job so he can afford a real ring?

No one else seemed to question this or wonder if their engagement was legitimate. For the rest of the night, the conversation sounded more like a class discussion one would have at Cambridge rather than regular people talking over dinner. It made me wish I had read more as a child and watched less *Saved by the Bell.*

At first, I had no appreciation for it, the feeling that I would forever and hopelessly be an outsider in England. I sat in the loneliness. Between my discouraging and desperate attempts to fit in, I spent a lot of time by myself. *Nobody gets me here . . . I can't understand my professor's Irish accent . . . I don't know how to find anything in these supermarkets . . . The kids all make fun of me . . . I don't even know what an Eton ring is.*

I was hesitant to make friends in England because of my feeling of being an outsider, so I thought maybe I could find comfort and companionship in Oxford with the city itself. This had worked for me when I lived in Oxford before. That semester in college I was going through my very first breakup. I was sadder than I had ever been, and I was lonely. Even though I was surrounded by American friends, some days I felt isolated and alone in my sadness and confusion. I went for long solitary walks with my headphones on, listening to Coldplay and feeling very melodramatic and sorry for myself. I hid in the city's alleys and parks. Bundled in a scarf and hat, I wandered all over. The city helped me forget. I would study the cobblestones and the old churches, older than any I'd seen back home. They told my hurting twenty-year-old heart important things about time. About the withstanding of it, the resilience of beauty.

That fall, all the leaves in Oxford went to die in this one little alley that lay between a charming residential street and Woodstock Road, which leads to the city center. I muddied the leaves with my feet, but they retained their colors. Bright red, bright orange, bright yellow. Even the leaves were resilient in this place.

It's important to find safety during a lonely or sad or hard time. I grew up believing God is our hiding place, and I believe he manifests this physically when we need it most. You stumble upon a portion of park or a riverbank and immediately you love it there. Something about it says this is your spot. It is safe and made for you. It's his hiding place but in physical form. How wonderful for him to provide such shelter, not just to sleep and eat in, but to be sad in, to hurt in, to wonder in. We need it. The aesthetics, the familiarity. We have to be reminded we are resilient creatures who have weathered much worse. These places do that for us.

I remembered that alley and the healing power of Oxford's streets during this second fall in England, when I was feeling a different type of pain and a different type of loneliness. I took walks with my headphones on, just as I had two years before. I returned to that little alley. I hoped if all else failed with actual people, the city and its buildings could be my friends.

I walked slowly and noticed the beautiful bits of Oxford, where the stone walls are thick, high, and unfathomably old. These structures seemed even more beautiful because of their suffering: bullet holes; corners disintegrated by wear, weather, and time. This city has been around since AD 912, meaning it has seen wars and every terrible thing a city can see in more than a thousand years. I knew those high walls had protected their citizens well for a long, long time.

On the other side of one wall on the north side of town, behind a gate, was University Parks, a park that stretched a mile wide and long and hid the River Cherwell in its eastern corner. If you knew where you were going, you could find a path just on the other side of the river that took you down the longest and most enchanting walk to a completely different part of the city, to a large grassy hill called South Park, where clusters of Brookes students sat and from a distance looked just like me and my college friends at home.

For a brief time, the city offered me its strong walls, resilient leaves, and ancient buildings, and they comforted me. Oxford hid me. It said I could wallow for a little while. I could disappear and walk for as many miles as I wanted, for it had miles to spare.

Soon though, I knew that exploring Oxford on my own was not

going to be enough to cure my loneliness. Not this time. People can tolerate loneliness for only so long. "We are born helpless," wrote C. S. Lewis. "As soon as we are fully conscious we discover loneliness. We need others physically, emotionally, intellectually; we need them if we are to know anything, even ourselves."[3] Maybe on Oxford's streets and alleys I was near other people, maybe I brushed shoulders with them and made the occasional eye contact, but as Lewis wrote, we don't simply need the proximity of other human bodies; we need people emotionally and intellectually as well. We need their attention. We need to have conversations with them and to feel at least an ounce of understanding in each other. It is without this that you can grow completely lonely surrounded by people in a city. It is without this that you can lose yourself if you're not careful.

My go-to method of hyper church involvement was not making me feel a part of this country, and neither were my sulking, solitary walks around the city. Friends were not going to come to me. Acceptance was not going to arrive on my doorstep. After a while when I finally woke up and realized I had made fifty acquaintances in Oxford, most of them from church, and zero friends, I knew it was time to do something. A layer of safety and comfort needed to be shed. So I got brave, really brave for that moment in time, and invited people from class—*heathen* friends, mind you—over for dinner. A small gesture that took everything in me.

I invited a small handful of people I knew from my Literary

---

3. C. S. Lewis, *The Four Loves* (Boston: Houghton Mifflin, 2012), 2.

Criticism class. I didn't know them well, but we had had the occasional postclass chats and even a couple of coffees together. They were not "church" people. They did not believe what I did, but I thought maybe looking for friends outside my church embassy could be good for me. I invited Sophie, the very first person I met at Brookes, and her boyfriend. I invited Ben, who was from England, and I invited Mac, who was from Philadelphia, the only other American in our class.

It was cold that night, and I remember feeling grateful they had made the trek to my house despite the weather. Sophie taught me how to cook curry in my ill-equipped kitchen while the guys hovered around. We ate in my living room with plates on our laps and talked and laughed for a long time. Mac brought chestnuts he had purchased from a street vendor, and we toasted them in a sauté pan to have for dessert, while Ben unwrapped Cadbury chocolate bars to break off and share. Curry, chestnuts, chocolate. It was an odd meal, but in the middle of it, I started to feel like myself again. I felt all wrapped up in the smoky aroma of the chestnuts. I felt like I might survive this country after all, maybe, and that the people who appeared to be nothing like me were actually a lot like me, and I was a lot like them. Maybe.

Eventually, a little while after that dinner, my solitary walks began to more frequently include other people, friends like Sophie and Ben and friends I met at St. Aldate's and elsewhere. I walked the city streets with someone beside me. I walked the path on the Thames while having a conversation. I noticed the beauty and the darkness of the water and the rustling in the trees and made comments about it to the people who were with me rather than taking the sights in alone. Companionship livened up an already beautiful landscape before me. It's amazing how people can do that.

But I had to take that first step toward others. I had to be willing to allow my lonely walks to be interrupted by the presence of someone else. The leaves and the streets and the buildings that fall, though lovely, turned out to be lousy friends.

Sometimes I think this world is a long and spread out Tower of Babel. You don't have to move to England in order to feel like a foreigner. It might feel like no one speaks your language in your own home, school, or workplace. The most familiar things in life can cause us to feel the loneliest at times. And loneliness is the absolute worst. But it can be effective at changing us for the better, forcing the layers off and allowing us to do brave things, appreciate relationships, and find friendships with people we didn't think we could befriend.

Submitting to Babel allowed me to feel connected to those around me. Before the dinner party, I thought I had to understand all the right words and phrases and had to de-Americanize myself in order to have anyone over to my house or in order to make real friends in England. Once I realized I could never get to this place, at least not until I was reincarnated as an English person, I could accept my ignorance and lack of knowledge and simply have people over for dinner. The first of many nights I had people over for dinner.

3

My Front Light

On a cold night in November, just before Thanksgiving, I walked into
The Eagle and Child. You know this pub. The Inklings—C. S. Lewis,
J. R. R. Tolkien, and others—made it famous, and much homage is
paid to them on the walls there. The Eagle and Child has small-paned
glass windows that are very storybook-esque. Their glow lures in the
passersby from the street, making them wonder what's inside. Its ceilings are low and threaten tall people like me. There are brick fireplaces
not in use, and it's a bit maze-like in layout. Instead of one large room,

there are several little rooms that lead in and out of each other—uncomfortable for those prone to claustrophobia but too charming to complain about.

I followed a long, dark wooden bar to the back, where my friend Gabriel and his party had set up camp.

My cycling buddy Gabriel was moving back home to France, and this was his going-away party. I had known Gabriel for only a few weeks, but a few weeks in Oxford, being the pressure cooker that it was, felt more like months, maybe even years. And so I considered Gabriel one of my good friends at the time.

We had adopted the routine of riding our bikes home from Sunday night church together. We lived in the same neighborhood, and I liked having a riding partner in the dark. I wondered who would cycle me home after Gabriel left.

I found everybody in the back room of the pub. I greeted Gabriel, who smiled big and excitedly. Gabriel had a running energy inside him, always threatening to escape. It made him light and springy, like Pooh's friend Tigger but with brighter eyes and an accent. I began the process of removing my winter clothing—gloves, coat, scarf, hat—and looked around at the others gathered in the room. It was dark. I squinted trying to make out everyone's faces.

Strangers, I could tell. Each one.

Gabriel and I didn't have many mutual friends, probably because we had only been friends since September. As this realization settled in, I began to feel silly for attending his going-away party. Going-aways are the type of party you attend when you really know someone, not when you've gone on a few bike rides together.

Going-aways are for going around the table and sharing what you love about your friend. Wrapping up mementos of the city your friend is leaving. Printing off a photo of the two of you together and having it framed. The strangers in this room had probably written cards full of sentimental language that recalled the good times they had had together and listed all the things they were going to miss about him. They had probably sealed the envelope and written Gabriel's name on the outside. The letters were sitting in their bags and pockets right now, waiting to be revealed at the perfect sentimental moment. Going-away parties are meaningful and special, so they should involve the special and meaningful people in that person's life. They should involve longer-than-normal hugging and making promises about visiting and keeping in touch.

I had no plans to visit Gabriel after he moved back home to France, and the words "meaningful" and "special" did not define the nature of our relationship. "Friendly acquaintance I ride my bike with sometimes" was more like it.

Gosh, I hardly knew the guy and was suddenly so aware of it now, at his going-away party. I looked around the table at the others, at the friends who had cards in their bags and were experiencing legitimate feelings of sadness, and I wondered, *Can they tell I'm not meaningful and special to Gabriel? Are they wondering who I am and why I'm here, as I am? Should I pretend to know him better than I do? Make up some memories of times we had together to share during the sharing portion of the evening? Should I just leave? Immediately?*

Most parties are come-and-go, but at good-bye parties the point is to stay until the end, right? So you can actually say good-bye?

I lowered myself hesitantly into a seat at the end of the long table, contemplating my departure. I kept my coat locked in my arms and my purse on my shoulder. My eyes continued to adjust to the darkness in the room, and then, unexpectedly, the person sitting to my left leaned over and introduced himself.

"What?" I said, startled. The pub was noisy, and it sounded like he said, "Hi, my name is Jesus."

"Did you say your name is Jesus?" I asked him.

"No." He laughed in a way that hinted this was not the first time someone had mistaken his real name for Jesus. "My name is Jisu. As in the letter *G* and the name *Sue.*"

"Oh, okay. Nice to meet you, G-e-e S-u-e," I said slowly, overarticulating. "I'm Andrea." I was still clutching my coat. I had not removed my purse. I wondered if "G-e-e S-u-e" was a meaningful and special person in Gabriel's life, and I wondered if he could tell from my unease that I was not.

"So," I said casually, "how do you know Gabriel?"

"I met him at the church I go to, St. Aldate's." This surprised me. I had never seen "Gee Sue" at St. Aldate's. I would have remembered.

"I go to St. Aldate's too! Gabriel and I always ride our bikes home together on Sunday nights." I said this with confidence, trying to justify my presence at the party. Trying to prove I was Gabriel's friend and not an imposter. That we did know each other, sort of.

"I do not know Gabriel very well, actually," admitted Jisu. "I only moved to Oxford a few months ago."

I looked at Jisu when he said this. He smiled, and when he did, his eyes scrunched until they disappeared. He looked very kind.

"I don't know Gabriel all that well either," I admitted back, relieved to have found another at the party like me. Only he was willing to be honest while I was trying to cover it up and fit in as best as possible. I liked Jisu's candor. It made me want to be candid too.

In contrast to some of the cold first meetings I had had with the British, Jisu was warm. Even in the dark lighting of that back room, with the fireless fireplace, I could sense an openness to him, a welcoming spirit. He looked right at me when I spoke.

Maybe I won't leave just yet, I thought. *Maybe I'll give Gabriel's going-away party a chance.*

I wanted to know more about this Jisu, his name and where he came from. When I asked, he settled in and straightened up with a deep breath, as if a PowerPoint presentation were about to appear behind him and a podium was going to rise up out of the floor. The answer to "Where are you from?" required some sort of speech.

Hands folded on the table in front of him, he began, "I am from Austria. But my parents are from South Korea and immigrated to Austria before I was born. So by nationality I am Austrian, and by blood I am Korean."

"That's an interesting combination. You hardly have an accent. I actually thought you were American when you introduced yourself."

"That is because I lived in Austin, Texas, for one year as an exchange student, and I lived in other places too, so my accent is improving."

"You lived in Austin?! I'm from San Antonio!" Other people at the table turned toward us, and I shrank back in my seat.

"We were neighbors," said Jisu. "And now, we meet here, in Oxford."

"Of all places."

"Of all places," he repeated.

My eyes had finally adjusted to the light, and I could see that Jisu was handsome. He had a good jaw, and his teeth were so straight and white. Exactly how we Americans like them.

"Where else have you lived?" I asked, choosing one of about one hundred questions I already had for him.

"Before Oxford, I was in Israel and Syria as a UN peacekeeper. I had a better tan than I do now." There was that kind-eyed smile. "I also traveled in Mexico after I lived in Austin, so I learned some Spanish." If you've been keeping count, so far we know Jisu speaks four languages. "I will begin French classes soon for my job. I need to relearn the French I knew in school." Four and a half.

Is this guy for real? I thought. Four and a half languages, a stint in Israel and Syria as a peacekeeper, a foreign-exchange student in America, a road trip through Mexico. He was twenty-seven years old. I was speaking with someone who knew a lot more about the world than I did, but he didn't brag about it, his worldliness. He was humble about his experiences, his travels, and his knowledge. I got the feeling he was even more accomplished than he was letting on.

"Have you found it easy to adjust to British life?" Jisu asked me.

"No, I feel out of place here a lot. I feel like I try too hard, with British people especially. I feel like I'm too much or something. Like too loud. And I'm not. Where I come from, people consider me pretty quiet and reserved."

"Yes, I like Americans for this," he laughed. "You are more open. I remember that. It would be difficult to live here if you are not from Europe. It is difficult for me, and I am from Europe."

We took sips of our drinks. The moment was refreshing. When you're in a new place, it's amazing how many consecutive days you can go without feeling or acting like yourself. You're trying hard to be who people need you to be, to make a good impression, to make friends. You don't even know how exhausted you are until you finally sit down beside someone familiar, or someone who at least feels familiar. It melts the exterior off you, allowing your body and limbs to move about freely again.

I remember the details of the room that night, the lighting, Jisu's pullover sweater and his smile, but I don't remember speaking to anyone else at the table. I know there were others there; I just can't remember who. I'm not even sure where Gabriel was sitting. Or maybe he was in a different room? After Jisu introduced himself to me, the purpose of the evening quickly shifted from saying good-bye to Gabriel to saying hello to this new person, this new friend.

It's interesting to think back on the first time you met a dear friend. What was it that pulled you toward that person? What was the nature of that first impression? What made it good? Why do we move toward some people so naturally and away from others? I don't know what it was exactly with Jisu. His smile, the mention of my home state of Texas, the complexity of his nationality. The sexy detail that he could speak French. Perhaps it was the ridiculously intimate ambience in that dark back room, where it felt like the ceiling would give way any minute and the unlit fireplace haunted my peripheral vision.

What is it ever, though, when you meet someone you already feel connected to? You know this is your first time meeting, but somehow you already know each other. It's clear. It's obvious, and it's comfortable. Small talk turns to real talk quickly, and it feels like you should already have inside jokes.

That type of connection. It's an understanding between you and him, and your eyes tell each other, *It's safe here. You already know me. It's safe.*

That was Jisu at The Eagle and Child, one night just before Thanksgiving. A stranger sat across from me and a stranger sat to my right, but to my left was an old new friend. A friend of Korean blood and Austrian origin, who spoke four-and-a-half languages and knew parts of the world in a way I did not.

After the festivities in the bar died down, we all filed out onto the sidewalk to say good-bye to Gabriel. Because, even though I had forgotten for a moment, it was his going-away party.

Jisu and I continued to talk standing under a streetlight that cast the pavement in a deep yellow glow. Under this light, I confirmed Jisu's attractiveness, and I noticed his height. He was tall—this was important—a smidge taller than me and well built.

He talked a little about his deep appreciation for Jewish culture and messianic practices. He was a rare breed in Oxford that we liked to call a "nonstudent." He had a job. He worked for a charity that helped inspire leadership skills in underprivileged youth. I assumed this job would be temporary because I know the wanderer type, and I could tell, not only from what he told me but also from how he looked, that he was the wanderer type. He didn't have dreads or a tattered backpack or anything. He was pretty clean cut, actually, but there was something in his eyes or maybe it was the way he thought for a long time before he spoke. Whatever it was, something let me in on what he was saying beneath the surface of his words and his stories: "I am a wanderer. I don't belong to any one place. I won't stay here for long, or anywhere for long. There's too much to see elsewhere and everywhere." When the world calls wanderers to leave, they always respond to the call, and it is best to let them go.

"What will you do for the Thanksgiving holiday?" he asked me.

"I think I'm going to go to a gathering at Wycliffe. I know some other Americans there who are putting on a big lunch that day." Wycliffe Hall is Oxford's evangelical theological college, and there are always a good handful of Americans studying there.

I paused after I said this. I thought about extending an invitation to Jisu, but I didn't. *Don't force your American holidays on everybody,* I told myself.

Instead, I turned to look for Gabriel, remembering once again that this was his party. I spotted him farther down the pavement in the middle of long, drawn-out hugs and conversations with some of the strangers. It was late and cold. I could have left without his noticing, but I was waiting around so we could cycle home together, one last time. He had promised me we would.

I was also maybe waiting around to see what my new friend was doing next.

Gabriel saw me looking and waved at me and Jisu excitedly, like Tigger. "We're going to another bar!" he said, sort of bouncing and pointing to the fellow French friends around him. His real friends.

I looked back at Jisu. He was zipping his coat and looking ready to leave. He did not seem particularly invested in spending the entire evening with Gabriel, our friend we had both known for several weeks now. This made me not invested either.

I walked toward Gabriel and shrugged my shoulders. "I think I'll just head home." Gabriel's expression turned pouty for half a second. Then he hugged me quickly and rushed off, trotting toward city center to catch up with the others.

I watched him go. *Good-bye, my French cycling buddy. I guess I'll be riding home alone now.*

I walked back to where Jisu was mounting his bike and bidding farewell to someone. He turned toward me, and I said good-bye. *It was nice to meet you. I feel like you're my best friend. Please be in touch with me like you said you would.*

I didn't say all that, but I thought it. I had a feeling we would be in touch. Because it felt like we had been in touch for a long time already.

Jisu promised to reach out, smiled, and said good night. The promise did not feel empty, and the good-bye did not feel final. He rode away from me, and I watched him go as his bike skipped in and out of the dim yellow puddles of light.

·◦∞◦·

Meeting Jisu was, as I had suspected, the beginning of something meaningful. After The Eagle and Child, we sent Facebook messages back and forth about how rare it was to be able to speak so freely with someone you'd only just met. He said he had "learned and shared" a surprising amount. I agreed.

A week later we met up to attend a Christmas party at St. Aldate's. We had both been invited, and we both didn't know anybody else who was going. Pioneering a new place with a friend on your arm makes you twice as brave as you would be alone. Jisu was the perfect brave companion for me in Oxford.

We rode our bikes together to the restaurant where the party was and walked in, side by side. One of the worship leaders at church introduced himself, and after chatting for a while he asked, "So how long have you two been together?"

My eyes went wide and I was too embarrassed to look directly at Jisu.

"Oh, we're not together," I said quickly. "I just met him last week."

And then I nervously laughed, and the worship leader apologized and changed the subject.

When Jisu and I left the party that night, we didn't say anything about it.

Our friendship formed with ease. Part of my draw to him—jawline and French aside—was the way he knew and loved God. It was different and maybe deeper than the way I knew God. Perhaps this happens when you are raised a Christian in the middle of Europe, a largely post-Christian society. This is why Jisu was a reprieve for me in the confusing city of Oxford and academia. He was a kind person to sit beside who shared my beliefs but perhaps believed them more than I did.

Every once in a while, my school friends and I liked to throw wine and cheese parties. They weren't really parties in the typical sense of the word. We would gather at Sophie's and her boyfriend's apartment. Mac and Ben were usually there and some other friends from school. We sat on the floor in the living room and gorged ourselves on crackers smeared generously with Brie. We passed around bottles of red and white, and I drank and scooped handfuls of nuts, pretending I knew what everybody was talking about when the conversation turned heady and academic. Pretending I liked red wine. (By the end of that year, I would have a love affair with the stuff, but not yet.) I nodded, crunched, and sipped. And sipped and sipped. After a few glasses, the conversation often turned to religion.

I remember one night standing in the kitchen waiting for my Brie to come out of the oven when I heard the others talking in the living room. "Religion is a nice thought for some people," someone said. "It makes them feel better. That's nice for them. It's comforting."

"Yeah, I agree . . . ," said everyone.

My face went hot, and I said nothing. I looked at the timer on the stove and hoped no one would remember I was the one religious representative of the group. I loved God, the Being they said it was "nice" to believe in.

Sometimes the conversation grew hostile. A couple of the guys, staunch in their atheism, prodded Christianity with harsh voices and words. Jokes I didn't like but sometimes laughed at anyway.

I was never very happy with my behavior during our wine and cheese parties. I should have been demoted from my religious representative role, but they kept me there, in spite of my silence, in spite of my laughter.

A lot of my memories of those first months in Oxford are cast in a dark light. Having been plucked out of southern America and then dropped there, I was startled by the contrast. One place had a church on every corner, and the other place had a church on every corner, but the churches were centuries old, and the pews inside were typically empty. As the home of *Oxford* Oxford and some of the most brilliant academic minds in the world, it is the type of place where people don't need religion. And I could sense this, the lack of need for God. It felt dark and sad, but it also made sense. Religion is merely comforting? Yes, it is comforting. Is that what we Christians are doing, comforting ourselves? Maybe. I liked believing in a Being who was taking care of me and guiding me, who had things under control, who would make everything work out in the end. In this sense, it was easier to believe in God than to not believe in him, which made me wonder if faith really was for the weaker species, as my friends said, as if we were somehow less evolved than the others who had learned to live without this teddy-bear God. It really is logical when you think about it, and my understanding of this logic and how quickly I was able to jump over to logic's side scared me.

So many nights in Oxford, especially the wine and cheese nights, I felt like none of the details of my faith were getting clearer. Instead, they were getting fuzzier. Nights turned restless with the questions and the thoughts.

I had gone through that brief season of doubt in high school, but this was different. That time, I felt distant from God. This time, I doubted his very existence, and the doubt was getting into my bones. I could feel it, like a cold numbness resistant to thaw.

My journal entries grew increasingly depressing during this time. I wrote this on December 29:

> I've never wanted or wished for ignorance, but right now I see the necessity of ignorance, in that it is bliss. Because if I were ignorant right now, ignorant to the fact that most people in

this world don't believe Jesus was God incarnate, ignorant to the realization that atheists can live happily and find joy and love without any concept of God, I wouldn't be having a constant apologetics debate in my head. It's seriously what it feels like. My believing side defending itself to my unbelieving side. I just don't know anymore, and I'm not sure how much longer I can live with uncertainty. Still everything comes back to God, but I've watched myself consider the alternative so much I'm becoming harder and harder. . . . I still cry out to God. I'm not giving up. I refuse to give up, but the questions, oh the questions are tough and numerous. So tough I fear writing them even here. I wish I was fourteen again, finally getting to know God and the Bible on my own, changing for God, becoming passionate about upholding my faith. Now it's much larger. It's choosing to believe in something. I don't want to slip away, but I don't know how to prevent that when my hand is grasping ice, melting and slick.

One night when I was riding my bike home from class I could suddenly feel for the first time what it would be like to be Godless. Just suddenly, in that random moment. My body, my heart—they felt it. I could sense the emptiness, the space it left in my world. I could see the blankness of it. A life without God. For the first time, it felt completely possible and not altogether terrible.

I had not been able to imagine that before. Maybe I thought I had. Maybe I had considered my brief periods of doubt equivalent to not believing at all, but they weren't. Not really. What I felt that night in Oxford, and subsequent nights, was real. And it was strikingly dark.

I've been so naive, I thought.

·⟶·

For as many wine and cheese nights as there were—or nights when the questions didn't stop and the Godlessness felt all too possible—for as many nights like that as there were, there were days with Jisu.

Whenever I met up with Jisu, I felt myself relax again the way I did the very first time we met. It was as if I had been holding my breath, holding it all in, and then suddenly sitting on a couch beside my friend with a mug of something warm in my hand, I could let it seep out. The breath. The truth of who I was. I could put aside the running dialogue in my head *(God is a comforting thought for me. It is nice to believe in him. It does make me feel better. Is that all it is for me? Maybe that's all it is for me . . .)* and not worry so much.

It's not that Jisu and I had deep conversations about apologetics or that we read the Bible together or prayed. We didn't do those things. We were just friends who hung out and talked like normal people, but something about his presence, something about his nearness brought the exact amount of encouragement I needed at that exact time.

When I couldn't, I knew Jisu talked to God. I didn't know this because he told me. I knew because in Jisu's spirit was a quietness and a steadiness. He was made up of something solid and possessed a firmness in his faith that I wanted and that I leaned on, whether I knew I was leaning on it or not.

·ᴄᴏ·

Until I arrived in Oxford, I had taken pride in a very individual and personal, somewhat private, faith. I had quiet times. I had good prayer times with my Jesus, and I hadn't relied much on others when it came to spiritual growth and understanding. I liked being by myself. I liked reading my Bible alone and learning things that I could tell others later. I liked coming to conclusions on my own. My faith became private to the point that anyone else coming along to "help" me would have felt like an interruption. I didn't need them. I had God. And God and I had had a good thing going since I was about fourteen years old. That's when I read through the Gospels for the first time and felt forever changed. Others need not mess that up.

I wonder if a part of my individualism came from my place in the church community, my role as the preacher's daughter. In the church of my childhood, and still today, there is a prayer time at the end of the service. Several members of the congregation, called "prayer partners," line the front of the auditorium, and the rest of the congregation is invited to come forward for prayer. No one told me I shouldn't go forward, but I didn't think I was allowed to. I never even considered it. Not once. What would people think if I, Andrea Lucado, went forward for prayer? They would think I needed help. They would think my prayer life was not strong enough on its own. They would think something was wrong with me or my family. I saved the prayer partners for those who were brave enough to be prayed over in public, and I kept my prayers, issues, problems, and concerns private. No one taught me to do this. It was just one of those lessons I had told myself over time—that as a member of my family, not only did I need to have my life together on the outside, but I needed to have my spiritual life together also. What was on the outside needed to match the inside. Going forward for prayer meant I needed a mediator between me and God. It meant that I, on my own, was not strong enough to talk to him myself. And that weakness, no matter how real and true it was, was not a side of me I was willing to show others. Not yet and not there, in my home church.

In Oxford, I maintained my private faith the best I knew how. I read my Bible, as was my morning habit. I did a Beth Moore Bible study. I journaled. I did the tasks, the writing, and the studying. The things I had been doing faithfully since I was fourteen years old. I could read, write, study. Those actions were not the obstacle for me there. It was the conversation part that was hard. In Oxford, my conversations with God were quieter. They felt strange, almost awkward, as if the God I was trying to talk to in England was not the same God I had always talked to back home in Texas. Our talks often felt one-sided. When I prayed, I hit dead ends. Was God disappearing as I began to imagine and understand life without him? Was I making him disappear? And if he was disappearing, how could I talk to a disappearing someone?

Maybe this is why I talked to Jisu more than I talked to God that year. Because at some point, your morning quiet times are finally so quiet they only echo your own voice back to you. "Anyone out there? Anyone out there? Anyone?" What you want instead, what you need, isn't God, but someone, a physical real-person someone, to show you the way. You want to talk to someone who you know is talking to God, even if you can't or just don't want to.

The people who talk to God can do a lot for you and for your faith if you let them. I once heard author and pastor Nadia Bolz-Weber speak. During the question and answer session at the end, a guy stood up and said, "I had faith and it was strong, but now I'm doubting. I feel weak in my faith. What should I do?"

Bolz-Weber's suggestion? "You can take a break now. Let someone else on the pew be strong for you."

I like this idea of giving each other permission to take a break from trying and let the others on the pew be strong for us for a little while. As you boomerang from one dead end to another, the stronger ones take you by your shoulders. Right where you are, facing that dark stone wall, they place their hands on you and gently turn you around to point you toward something bright, toward something true. I have a name for these people who are nice enough to take me by my shoulders and point me in the direction I should go. I call them my "front lights," and I'll tell you why.

One cold and dark night in Oxford, I was the victim of a theft.

To ride a bike legally in Oxford, you are required to have a headlight and a taillight. Or as we called them there, front lights and back lights. These lights were hot commodities for thieves, who I suppose sold them or added them to some strange Ariel-esque collection of worthless trinkets in their cupboards. To keep the thieves away, it was important to own detachable lights so that whenever you left your bike, you could take your lights with you and then reattach them when you returned. It sounds like a lot of effort to go through, but it was one of those things that everybody did, so I did it too.

One night, when out at a pub, I forgot to take my lights inside, and I didn't remember them until we were walking out to leave.

"My lights!" I yelled. "I forgot to take them off. Do you think someone stole them?" I ran to where I had parked my bike. The lights were still there. Still attached, in the same place I had left them.

"No one stole my lights!" I exclaimed.

"Oh, that's a relief," my friend said. I got on my bike and flipped on my lights. Nothing happened. I tried again. On. Off. On. Nothing.

"Did it burn out?" I asked.

"Must need new batteries."

"Hmm . . ." I opened the battery compartment and inside I found only one battery where there should have been two.

My lights had not been stolen, but someone, apparently in desperate need of a single AA battery, had swiped one from my front light.

"Someone stole a single battery from me?" I looked at my friend in disgust.

It would have been better if they had taken the entire thing. Instead, they took the time to remove my light, open the compartment, take one battery out, and then reattach my light. It felt weird, and intrusive. Like someone had dug through my underwear drawer and then put it all back. I felt violated. I felt annoyed.

"Who would do that?" I asked rhetorically.

"I don't know; that is really odd. I guess you'll just have to buy some new batteries."

My friend was clearly not as bothered as I was.

"No," I said, shocked at her suggestion. "He should pay for it. The thief should pay." Though I didn't see it, I'm sure my friend rolled her eyes as she rode away.

I remained defiant about the battery for weeks. Refusing to buy a new pack, and simply forgetting to buy them each time I went to the store. Mechanically I would reach down to flip my front light on, forgetting it needed a battery, and then I'd remember. Each time I did this I got angrier at the mysterious battery thief. It was an unhealthy cycle that had a simple solution, but I chose to keep it complicated.

My front light being out bugged Jisu. He didn't think it was safe for me to ride without it, so for a few weeks, he always rode in front of me at night.

"I'll be your front light," he told me.

"Oh, I'll be fine. I don't need one."

"Andrea, it's illegal not to have one, and you won't be able to see." He was right, so for a few weeks, I surrendered. Any time we were out somewhere together at night, he would ride in front of me. It was uncomfortable at first. Independence isn't just an issue I have with my faith. I felt bad that he would go out of his way just to ride his bike in front of me until I got home or that he would wait until I was ready to leave just so I could have a light to guide me. But after a while, I got used to it. I even liked it.

One night when I was leaving Jisu's house, he loaned me his head-lamp to be my front light. He put it on me, stretching it over my wool beanie, and standing very close to me. I made my old arguments.

"I'll be fine. I don't need it this time. Really. Is it even legally con-sidered a front light if it's attached to my head?" He ignored me and smiled, tightening and adjusting until it felt just right.

"I feel ridiculous. Do I look ridiculous?" He didn't answer and despite my self-consciousness, I didn't take it off. He was probably wondering why this American girl couldn't just buy some batteries already, but even if he was thinking that, he didn't say it out loud. He didn't make me feel guilty or ridiculous. He simply gave me his headlamp.

Jisu even texted me before class one night, "Do you need me to come get you after class tonight? To be your front light?"

My school sat at the top of Headington Hill, and Headington Hill was admittedly steep, not a hill you would want to attempt in the dark. Of course picking me up after class meant riding *up* Headington Hill, which was about a mile long. This didn't deter Jisu from offering.

I don't think my French cycling buddy, Gabriel, would have of-fered to pick me up from class at the top of Headington Hill. Jisu was a far superior riding buddy.

Jisu, my front light.

·〰·

I think if the sun suddenly shut off and you took an aerial shot from space of a crowded street anywhere in the world, you would see a mix of front lights and the people who follow them. The ones holding the front light saying, "Hey, I've been there. I've done that. Follow me." And you would see the followers, the ones following the light carriers, holding the hand of the friend in front who waits patiently and faithfully.

Even when it looks like it, even when it feels like it, no one is really doing this faith thing alone. No one can do it alone. We simply wouldn't be able to find our way. Not without our front lights; not without being a front light for someone else.

Around the time of that other journal entry, I also wrote this: "It's the faith of other people that is keeping mine alive right now." I thought it was wrong for me to confess to this and write this, even to my own journal. But really, I was onto something.

Sometimes faith comes very naturally, and sometimes everything we've ever believed is suddenly thrust under a microscope and we are forced to examine it. It's okay to look. In fact, please look. Because if you don't, what are you looking at instead?

I like what Oswald Chambers says about this: "Always make a practice to stir your own mind thoroughly to think through what you have easily believed. Your position is not really yours until you make it yours through suffering and study."[4]

So suffer. Study. And find a front light.

4. Oswald Chambers, *My Utmost for His Highest,* ed. James Reimann (Grand Rapids: Discovery House, 1992), December 15.

I should have, but I didn't take Jisu up on his offer to ride with me home from class. I rode down alone, hoping no one would catch me riding illegally, hoping there were no invisible potholes in my path, relying only on the sporadic puddles of yellow light projected by streetlamps, ignoring a little corner of my psyche and my heart that wished Jisu were riding ahead of me.

4

The Atheist Society

Ben came to Christmas Eve service with me, so it was my turn to go to the weekly Atheist Society meeting with him. The Atheist Society was a group of Oxford students who gathered around their common disbelief in God. The society was mostly made up of *Oxford* Oxford students, but they accepted students like us, who went to Brookes. Ben was a member and attended faithfully, just as I attended St. Aldate's. In 2009 the official name for this group was the Oxford Atheist Society, but in 2010 they merged with the Oxford Secular Society to form a group called Oxford Atheists, Secularists and Humanists. When we attended and when Ben was a member, it was just the good ole Atheist Society, so that is what I will call it.

When I met Ben in one of my classes at Brookes, I didn't expect us to become friends. He was not like the guys I knew at school back home. He was a devout atheist. He was reserved, quiet, watchful, in a way that made me wonder what was going on in his head. He told me once that he wasn't a big fan of daylight. Daylight in general, that is. Like, the sun. He didn't really like the sun. This was during the height of the *Twilight* frenzy, so for a very brief second, I wondered if Ben was a vampire.

A lot about him was very mysterious to me. He was in the middle of writing a young adult novel about something that sounded smart. He didn't feel the need to act cooler than he was, and he didn't feel the need to turn in papers on time or worry about his grades. He was a trained pianist, and his side job that year was as a reader for a girl in our class who was blind. Each week he read aloud to her whatever required reading she had. Required reading for our course was a few hundred pages per week, so that sounded like the worst job in the world to me and, therefore, elevated Ben to saint status.

Right away Ben was kind to me. He laughed at my jokes that weren't funny. He seemed genuinely interested in me, where I came from, what I was about. He invited me to meet up with him for coffee before class. He was the first person I met at school to whom I confided my faith. By the way he reacted, with a smile and genuine curiosity, I knew Ben was a safe person I could share with. I knew I could be myself around him.

In mid-December I invited several of my school friends to the St. Aldate's Christmas Eve service. Ben was the only one who showed up. He wanted to hear the music.

"I hope you play 'In the Bleak Midwinter,'" he told me. "That's my favorite hymn."

Of course it is, I thought.

I think church lived in a strange place in Ben's heart, somewhere between love and disdain. He had played the piano for his church at home, a church he began to attend after he became a Christian at age sixteen and a church he quit attending after he decided he was no longer a Christian at age eighteen. I never knew the Christian version of Ben. I only ever knew the atheist version, but I think both are equally kind, open, listening, and accepting. And both would have spent hours a week reading to a blind student.

In the winter, in the dark, in our coats, Ben and I met up at a pub in the center of town for my first Atheist Society meeting. My attendance was comical, but only to me and Ben. The others had no idea who I was or how much I didn't belong. I think that was the thing—no one didn't belong at the Atheist Society meetings. They didn't check names at the door or seem to really care if you were a true atheist or not. It was simply a social gathering, an opportunity for students to meet other students, like a Campus Crusade for Christ event or a Young Life event, only smaller and without music and religion. And instead of meeting in a classroom or a church, we were in a bar. We did, however, have games.

Upon arrival, we broke off into teams for an atheist-themed pub quiz. For one of the questions, we had to draw an imagined Darwinian species that might live one thousand years from now. We were to use our imaginations and give it a name, and then we would share it with the other groups. Ben and I basically drew a circle and then slapped on every animal appendage we could think of: fins, tails, hooves, claws, wings. Our poor, ugly, nameless Darwinian creature. We didn't win that question, but somehow, even though we were a team of Brookes students and one of us was a Christian, we won the overall quiz. We laughed about our ironic victory all the way home.

The president of the society was a spunky auburn-haired girl who was in her final year at Oxford. She wore a denim skirt over leggings. The skirt was a size too tight for her, in my opinion, but I admired her confidence. I wondered about her as she got up to give announcements. I liked her. She was vibrant, a natural leader. I saw her once, weeks later, walking down a sidewalk when I was leaving a coffee shop. I almost ran her down to say hi. She seemed like the type who would have liked that, but I didn't do it.

During the Atheist Society meeting, I thought a lot about my potential involvement with the group. Should I come again? Should I be a member? Would people be friends with me here? Would I come with the intent to evangelize? Would it be wrong if I did? Would it be wrong if I didn't? In that room I felt the need to be accepted by those around me. The same need I felt in any other room of people I also felt here with those I had considered to be the most opposite of me. Perhaps I even felt it more strongly with the society of atheist people. I wanted them to see me beyond my religion, yet I knew that at my core I was my religion.

My religion. What did it look like to them? Maybe they considered it something you grow out of. Maybe they, like Ben, thought Christianity is the result of passionate, emotionally stimulating conferences that have little or nothing to do with actual life, that will fade once you get home and go to church and see only dead souls in alive bodies sitting on the pews. And that, like Ben, after a couple of years, you close the cover to the piano one last time and walk out the door.

The church of my teen years looked nothing like the church of Ben's teen years. Mine was a gym-turned-auditorium with room for eighteen hundred people. Golf carts carried people from their parking spaces to the building's doors. Hundreds of others my age were there sharing what I believe, trying to be good, then messing up on Saturday nights and trying to be good again until we finally started to get it— that it actually has nothing to do with doing or good.

I rode in my mom's car every Sunday morning, fighting with my sisters about who was wearing my sweater without asking me first and begging my mom to let me wear my favorite brown lipstick. Donut glaze still sticking to my fingers, I dialed my friends' numbers to make sure they were saving me a seat in the back, with our other friends. I stayed after service until the lights were turned out. And when I got bored, I looked for my parents and my sisters to find out where we were going to lunch and how soon we could leave. We all did it. Everyone significant in my teen years went to church, either with me to mine or with their families to theirs. Either way, family and friends were there.

How different this must have been for my kind friend Ben. He grew up in a city north of Oxford, where he attended a small church. The church looked like what you might think a church would look like in the English countryside. Small, stone, and old with weathered gravestones in the yard. He told me he had become a Christian at a camp. He went home thrilled with this new discovery of Jesus. He began to attend the old stone church. He played the piano during service. He attended for as long as he could but found few others there who were like him. Most were older, much older, and seemed to attend only because it was what they did more than because it was what they believed.

I wonder if Ben arrived at church alone and left alone. I wonder if it took a long time or any time at all for the high of the camp to wear off and the reality of religion in an English village to set in. I wonder what it was he needed that he lacked. Was it more faith, or was it more faithful people around him? I wonder if the preacher at his church asked Ben any questions. If he or she tried to get to know him. If anyone there cared about who he was, or if they simply liked his piano playing. I wonder if anyone knew his name.

I wonder what it was like for him that day, the day he closed the piano and walked out the wooden church doors for the last time.

I volunteered at a Christian summer camp right after college. I remember one night a camper approached one of the other counselors, very concerned for his girlfriend.

"Sally lost her faith," he said. Shaking his head, distraught.

"What? She lost her faith?" the counselor asked.

"Yeah. It's just, it's gone. She doesn't believe anymore."

On the final night, the emotional skit night that gets kids all revved up and even more emotional than their teenage selves already are, that same guy approached the counselor again, excited this time.

"Sally got her faith back!"

"What?" the counselor asked.

"Her faith! It's back!"

If Sally's boyfriend had only known Ben, someone who actually did manage to "lose his faith," the story would have been problematic for him, as it was for me.

At Christian summer camp what you hear most are accounts of teenagers who become Christians at a camp just like the one you are at, teenagers whose lives are changed from drinking and drugs to Jesus. Now, here they are, preaching at camp. You hear about the success stories. You don't hear about the tragic ones as often, the failures. The kids who had a moment and accepted Christ and then went home and felt alone and couldn't help but feel betrayed.

I didn't want that to be Ben's story. We don't want that to be anyone's story. It means that we failed. It means that we're not foolproof in this conversion thing. And I think right now I'm supposed to blame Ben and say it was him. He was the one who never believed in the first place. But the problem with that is, I know Ben. Well, I knew Ben, and he was smart and he was not gullible and he was not the type to be swept up into something if he hadn't thoughtfully considered it first. He was not Sally, feeding off the drama of Christian church camp. For him, believing in Christ was as conscious and well-thought-out a decision as un-believing in Christ was later.

The arguments we have about these "faith failures" hold up only until you are friends with said faith failures. It's easy to say things are one way or another until you become friends with someone who is not one way or another, but rather somewhere in between. The labels we like to slap on people from a distance begin to peel off as we get closer to them.

It was interesting though. Ben didn't have the bitter edge I thought he should have. Christianity had failed him. We Christians had tricked him into believing something that wasn't true, and then we weren't even nice enough to convince him, this eighteen-year-old kid, to stick around. Even though I represented and championed this establishment he had walked away from, Ben was a good and consistent friend for me in Oxford. Whenever we met up in the cafeteria for coffee before class, he always wanted to discuss my latest blog post. He was the most avid reader of my blog, aside from my parents, and his enthusiasm encouraged me to keep writing. It was Ben who introduced me one morning to the British breakfast delicacy of beans on toast. We suffered through Shakespeare lectures together. We sat at the Oxford library side by side. I worked on papers for class while he edited his novel. We had conversations over wine and cheese about religion and lots of other things. And, of course, we boasted for weeks about winning the quiz at the Oxford Atheist Society.

Yes, Ben was a good friend, but he puzzled me. I could not figure out where he fit. I had my categories of people and where they are in their walks of faith, and he was not defined by any of those. He had gone rogue. He had created his own path away from mine.

Ben was a Christian anomaly, a creature with no name.

I didn't understand. Who could learn the teachings of Christ and not hold fast to them? Who sees this thing, the Cross, where all your bad and dirty, disgusting, terrible and shameful parts have gone to die so that you rise up from being flat on your face a completely new person—who experiences that and says, "No, no thank you"? How does it not stick, take hold, transform? What goes wrong? What synapse forgets to send the message of eternity and wholeness and purity, justification, redemption? Where is the link that went missing?

What happened to Ben? What happens to so many others? The ones who felt the warmth of light but said they prefer the cold of darkness. That they prefer it to sunlight.

I wish I could tell you, but I don't know. I have no theological response for you. All I know from Ben and his story is that people are more complicated than we want them to be. No one can ever live up to the names we give them.

Other people are not us. They did not go to church each Sunday in a gym-turned-auditorium with room for eighteen hundred. They didn't all have friends to call to make sure they were saving them seats. Each person we know has gotten to where he or she is via a different route than our own. The people who raised them, the things they saw, the lessons they learned, they are different from our experiences. And while we cannot expect everyone to get into our heads and understand us, we can try to get out of our own, at least for a minute or two, and understand others. It's not easy. It takes practice, time, and concentration. It does not come naturally for us, we quick-to-categorize-and-slow-to-understand types. But I think if we knew and believed in the complicated layering that is each and every one of us, more Christians would befriend atheists, and more atheists would befriend Christians. More "others" would befriend their own "others," in all categories.

Today, I think I do understand Ben a little better than I did then. I get the appeal of darkness. I have lived entire days, weeks, and months choosing it over light. I get not being a fan of sunlight. I get that. But somewhere along the way, light took up residence in me. It said, "I'm here and I'm not going anywhere, no matter how many times you shove me down and choose something less, something cold, something devoid." It has been persistent with me, and I'm not sure why, but I'm grateful it has.

As we are prone to do with things we don't understand or are afraid of or that threaten what we know to be true, slowly I began to let go of Ben. I released him without knowing. When the weather stopped being freezing cold and I was feeling more settled into Oxford and its rhythm, I stopped calling Ben as much, and then when classes were over, I stopped seeing him altogether. The unsolvable puzzle. The uncategorizable. The unbeliever. The "un" to all of my "how it should be."

One of the last times I saw Ben, he was leaving the library. I saw him clearly, but he couldn't see me. He was several yards away and walking in the other direction. I should have said "hi" or "hey" or "wait up" or something, but I couldn't. I didn't go after him. I let him walk away, and I stood still and watched.

The only thing I knew to do with Ben was nothing at all.

5

The Faith of Our Fathers

Beliefs, convictions, morals. They are ice cubes in our hands. If we hold them too tightly, if we bury them in our palms and wrap our fingers around them, they melt. We think we're protecting them, but we're not. We melt them with our ignorance and refusal to see both sides of an argument. We melt them ourselves and can't blame an unhappy circumstance or a friend who was a bad influence when we look down and our hands are dripping.

I held many ice cubes when I arrived in Oxford, and it took no time at all for them to melt away. Another country, another culture, new friends with unfamiliar beliefs and morals—they were warm breath blown on my precious truths and how-it-should-be's.

One night when Oxford was still new, I went to a housewarming party for an acquaintance from church. There I met a guy who was in Oxford to study apologetics for the year. I cornered him. In the living room for several minutes, maybe an hour, I drilled this guy about why I should believe what I believed. At the time I had become very preoccupied with this question: Would I still be a Christian if I had not been raised in a Christian home?

"What I'm struggling with," I said to the guy, "is that no one at my school is a Christian. Or it feels that way. My friend Ben, who I meet up with for coffee before class, asked me all these questions about being a Christian, and he seemed so interested, and then he said that he had converted to Christianity at sixteen and two years later renounced his faith. How does that happen? And his arguments? They make sense. And I don't like that. I don't have anything smart to say back. Everyone here is smart, and they know all these things and have read all these books, and I'm over here like, 'Hey guys. My dad's a preacher, and I'm a Christian, but now that you're asking, I'm not really sure why, and I'm not really sure if I would be a Christian today if I hadn't been raised as one—'"

"So," my new friend kindly interrupted, "I can see that you have a few questions about . . . things. Why don't you come with me to one of my lectures this week?"

"Seriously? Am I allowed? I would love to," I said as if I were talking to the cool girl at school who had just invited me to her birthday party.

"Yeah, sure. You can come. I have one this Thursday morning at nine."

"Oh, I will be there! Thank you so much. That's exactly what I need—an apologetics lecture. I'll learn everything I need to know. Thank you, really. I can't wait."

"Yeah, me either." He smiled, backing away. "See you Thursday."

The lecturer that Thursday turned out to be John Lennox, one of the most renowned apologists in the world. At *Oxford* Oxford, he was a math professor, but he also lectured at the Oxford Center for Christian Apologetics, where my friend from the party was studying. The class was held in the basement of an old building that looked like a big house across the street from University Parks in north Oxford. I had to walk downstairs to find the classroom. That's all it was. A small room with a few rows of desks and windows up high near the ceiling—an unassuming venue for someone of Lennox's caliber.

I spotted my friend from the party sitting at a desk in the middle of the room.

"Hey!" he said waving me over. "I saved this desk for you."

"Thanks," I said, still a little breathless from my bike ride over. I looked around. "Are you sure it's okay I'm here?"

"Yeah, yeah. Sure. I told Professor Lennox you were coming. He's fine with guests."

"Oh, okay. Well, good. I brought things to take notes." I laid out my pens and opened my notebook. I was prepared to write down everything this man had to say. I was prepared to learn all about why I was a Christian and how to defend my faith.

Lennox walked into the room, and everyone quieted down. He was bald on top with dark eyebrows. His dress was casual, and nothing about his appearance was overly intimidating. He didn't seem to notice an outsider in his class, and he made pleasantries with the students in the front row. I sat poised, pen in hand. Brain ready to absorb. He began.

During the hour, Lennox homed in on one takeaway point: we can indeed prove the existence of God using science. We do not need to step away from academics for a moment in order to find him. He can be proven using the same knowledge that disproves him every day. That's all I remember. Today that is all that is left from the lecture given by this famous apologist. It was the closest I will probably ever be to someone of his academic stature. I don't know where that notebook is in which I was so furiously taking notes. I don't remember why we can prove God's existence with science. I don't remember which part of science he used that day to prove it. Or maybe he used an equation? What I do remember is walking away from that classroom confident that someone much smarter than I am felt certain we could prove God's existence and that we had. What helped me that day, more than the details of the lecture, was a man who had gone before, who had asked these same questions and had somehow logically found the answers. And this confidence that lay in someone else's confidence comforted me greatly.

Well before the Lennox lecture, the first man who gave me this type of confidence in my faith was my father. My dad. My first pastor. "He has the gift of faith," my mom always says. It's true. His beliefs are steady, and I realize now how much hope my father's faith gave me in those young, formative years.

As a little girl I used to study my dad's hands during church before he got up to speak. I would run my finger along his calluses and comment on how dry his skin was. His hands felt enormous compared to mine, wrinkled, strong. Ugly, really. Compared to my mom's delicate hands, which I also loved to study, my dad's hands were not pretty. Yet looking at them, holding them, studying them—it comforted me. It comforts me now to even think about them, and that they probably look the same. Perhaps there are more calluses and wrinkles. I know they are still dry.

When I was young, his hands could have swallowed mine in a fist, and I imagined my whole body could have been held tightly in them, protected. When I didn't understand how God could hold the whole world in his hands, I understood how my father could hold me in his. His hands were big enough and strong enough. I understood that.

Our childish theologies are formed by pictures of our fathers, whether our fathers are present or not, kind or not. My father was comforting. This is why my faith grew so dependent on my dad's. Not because he stood at the pulpit each day, but because I would stare at his hands and examine them before he did.

John Lennox is a brilliant man who helped me and, I'm sure, the others who took his class, but my confidence in my father's faith is different; it's sturdier. I rely on it more often than the Lennox arguments I vaguely remember, and I wonder, *Is this okay? To rely so much on my father's, my pastor's, faith? Is it okay to be a Christian because I was raised in a Christian home?*

I once overheard a friend in Oxford say, "It's a form of child abuse for parents to force their own religious beliefs on their children." This was so shocking to me. I had always been grateful to have been brought up by Christian parents. I had not felt abused because we read the storybook Bible at night and listened to *Adventures in Odyssey* on cassette tape. I felt loved because of these things. I can see how someone who has not experienced the hope of the gospel might feel teaching Christian faith to children is imposing, maybe even harmful, but if you believe Jesus saves you, wouldn't it be wrong to not share that with your children?

Saying I'm a Christian because my father is a Christian was no argument for my atheist and agnostic friends in class, yet it was the argument I had those months in Oxford, maybe that entire year. It is the argument I have at times today when I feel God more closely and more intimately and I have a harder time disbelieving him than believing. Is it a weakness? To rely on the faith of those who have gone before us, to rely on the faith of our fathers? If you are like me, does it make us weak?

I used to think so. If we are all a bunch of people dependent on the faith of our fathers, who are dependent on their fathers, who are dependent on their . . . then who actually believes? I would ask this and spiral into a dark and doubting place, push the thought aside, and try to move on with my day. It was one of those gnawing questions I was embarrassed to ask aloud.

Today when I think back on that year and see how desperately I clung to my faith inheritance, I don't see it as a hole or weakness. Instead, it reminds me of something: how Christians have always been since the beginning of the church. This reliance and dependence began to look like God's design for us, rather than a coping mechanism or a scrambling attempt at belief.

The early church began not long after Christ's death. The early church members were close to Jesus; maybe some had seen him pass through their towns or perform a miracle. Perhaps one guy told a few friends about his eyewitness account of Jesus, and then those friends multiplied into a crowd, which turned the first guy into their leader, their pastor. He was simply relaying what he knew to be true to those who then relayed it to others. Until eventually, the church was just a group of people relying on each other, passing down information, remembering, believing, and encouraging. This is not weak or wrong. This is the church. I don't think we're called simply to rely on each other for comfort during the hard times or guidance during the confusing times. We're called to rely on each other for faith in general. When we don't know why or how to believe, we ask someone who believed before we did, and they remind us again of what is true and what our ancestor's ancestor's ancestor saw.

I remember Ben making the argument with me that if Jesus was the Son of God, why did we all have to go to church every Sunday to remind each other of that?

"Isn't that what church is?" he asked. "A bunch of people affirming each other in their beliefs. If it's true and God and Jesus are real, why do you have to remind each other of that once a week?"

It was a valid point. It was the type of observation I would have made if I had not been a Christian for so long. At the time, his question was unnerving, but today, I would tell him, yes, exactly. That's the entire purpose of church.

Think about all the lessons we are taught and believe because our teachers in school taught them to us. I trust grammar. I trust biology. I trust physics and chemistry and geometry because they were taught to me, their methods trusted and passed down for centuries. When Ben asked about the purpose of church, he was asking a much bigger question. He was asking why humans must gather and remind each other of truth, why we must pass it down and teach and reteach and relearn. He was asking, Why must humans rely on each other? And I ask, How could we not?

What we hear in church today is a passing down of scenes witnessed more than two thousand years ago. Our memory of that time has faded, so we need help to remember. Legacy is our memory keeper, and the church is our memory refresher. It's true that we have the Holy Spirit. And he is alive in us, yes. And no, we weren't left to our own devices. We have this Helper. But we also have our sin nature and an Enemy that is alive, well, and roaming. We have these things that work against our memory so that by Monday morning we have forgotten him, Christ, who he is and what that means for us.

And during our week, we function in this cloud of remembering and this desire to forget. We move and walk forward in this confliction and show up to our church, however that looks on whatever day that takes place and whatever place it takes place in, and we ask our pastors to remind us. We beg our friends beside us to teach us again who Jesus is, and as we listen to the words or the songs or see the Scripture in front of us for the first time in days, we begin to let Jesus resettle into us. We begin to remember why, when, and how. The death, the Resurrection, the stuff that all actually happened—the truth of it drips slowly into our cups, and we take a sip and remember, and we take another sip and remember, unaware of our thirst until that moment. Our children around us watch and see, and some of them know, and some of them will know someday soon, but we don't leave them out; we don't dare leave them behind. We all drink deeply, and we know. We know because our fathers passed down a faith that was passed down to them by their fathers, and those fathers had friends who were friends of Jesus, friends who saw and told the stories that are retold to us. The story hasn't changed, and what was written holds true.

6

A Spoon in My Tea

Though Oxford as a city felt a little spiritually dead to me, especially during winter, it is a city that appears very holy. With its old churches still standing and its rich history in the faith, the holiness of Oxford is a notch above the rest. And for Lent, the church's most anticipated season, it was an incredible place to be.

Lent took over Oxford in a holy way. An ancient practice taking place in an ancient city—there was something special about this Lenten season. You could feel it in the city's walls, in the frozen grass in South Park, in the air turned so very cold. In the snow that lay on the ground in my backyard. Oxford's streets went somber. Its very ground sat still in reverence. The snow remained for weeks, holding out and holding out and holding out. No new life yet. The city covered itself in a thin layer of mourning fog and holy fasting. The Oxford college chapels held nighttime choir concerts in their naves. In our church we recited the respectful liturgy, and our mouths moved in unison, our voices all swirled into one that went upward.

Yes, Oxford during Lent was an incredible place to be if you were cognizant enough, awake enough, or alert enough to be aware of it.

But I wasn't. I hated Lent that year. And I hated Oxford during Lent.

I, who decided to fast from caffeine for those forty days plus Sundays, did not walk around in the wonderment of the season. I did not appreciate the traditional hymns I heard coming from inside the college chapels—chapels I passed by while grumbling insane thoughts to myself that arose from a caffeine-deprived mind and body. The snow did not feel like a holy misting on the city. It was cold and it irritated me and forced me into shops, where I stood grudgingly to thaw my hands with my breath.

And my toes, oh my toes during that season were so perpetually half-numb, and I wore my enormous down coat and my thick wool hat every single day. Every day I was blanketed and covered, blowing on my fingers and forgetting why I had ever left south Texas. It seemed so senseless on those miserable, cold nighttime bike rides home in February and March. March no better than February. March giving me no relief or reason to have faith that spring would indeed come as it always did. March, instead, gave me an eerie sense that I had stepped into the winter part of Narnia, and there would be no Aslan to melt the snows away.

During my study-abroad semester in Oxford, I took a class called Oxford Through the Ages, where we walked around the city a couple of times a week and stopped at various historically significant places to learn about them. One of those places was the cathedral at Christ Church college—the beautiful glowing building you see on all the Oxford postcards. The cathedral at Christ Church has holiness built into its walls. Holiness and history, which are the same, I guess, when you're talking about cathedrals. This cathedral was arguably the most-discussed and rigorously tested Oxford site we visited for the class. Oxford's patron saint, Saint Frideswide, is buried there, and a stone shrine marks her resting place. Near the shrine are three long and tall pieces of stained glass. Each pane tells a different part of her story, her legend. Frideswide. The patron saint.

I was reminded of this Frideswide character when I attended a Christmas service at Christ Church, right before my unholy Lent. The lessons about her returned to me vaguely as we sat and recited liturgy and watched a priest scuttle from this place to that. Raising his hands, putting them back down. This is probably not true, but I imagine old Saint Frideswide to be a harsh woman with wide hips and a narrow face. Her character the opposite of Aslan's. Stiff and cold, like someone who actually enjoys winter. For this, sitting there in her dedicated cathedral, I began to resent her. I began to blame her for the winter, as if her ghost haunted the town still and determined whether or not spring could come.

During the Christmas service at Christ Church, I sat on an uncomfortable wooden chair that rested on a stone floor built in the eighth century. The walls to my right and left had witnessed church history unfold between them. I should have closed my eyes in awe and felt grateful. I should have sung with something deep inside me, some sort of reverence. To sit there was an honor. People made pilgrimages to that very place, simply to attend a service. But instead, there I sat, unappreciative, hallucinating about Oxford's patron saint.

Aside from Saint Frideswide and uncomfortable chairs, all I remember from the cathedral service is darkness and cold and blurs of red robes quickly walking past us, letting out very high-pitched sounds.

I can't help but wonder if the ghost of Saint Frideswide disapproved of my irreverence at the Christmas service, where she undoubtedly observed me from her high and mighty seat in the beautiful stained glass. I wonder if her ghost followed me home that night and then haunted me a little bit during my unholy Lent, her image everpresent in my subconscious. That stern face and tilted head, illuminated by a halo, looking down upon me in judgment for my lack of holiness, making everything just a tad colder than it already was.

When I chose to fast from caffeine, my coffee addiction was relatively new. It had begun two years before, when I was a junior in college. That's the year I learned to make real coffee in a real coffeemaker. At age twenty, making coffee in a coffeemaker and then pouring it into a big ceramic mug each morning made me feel very grown up, like I was really in my twenties.

Drinking coffee was all about appearances at first. Holding the mug. Standing in the kitchen with the mug. Pressing it against my cheek like my mom used to do. Eventually, after many consecutive days of making and drinking my regular coffee that was not iced or pumped with syrup, I acquired a taste for the actual flavor of the stuff. And once I acquired a taste for the real thing, it seemed I could never have enough. (Red wine, now that I think about it, has this same effect.)

One cup of coffee in the morning quickly became two cups in the morning. And then two cups in the morning became two cups in the morning plus one in the afternoon, and in less than a year, I was a three-cups-a-day coffee consumer. I didn't even think about it. The addiction was robotic. Around three in the afternoon my feet simply began to walk to the nearest coffee shop. They still do. It happens subconsciously. It is not a choice.

I tell you, it is not a choice.

My addiction became embarrassingly obvious in Oxford because no one shared it with me. I think the British, after all these years, are still wary of coffee. In my observance at least, the addiction has not quite swept them up like it has so many of us in the States. Sometimes I even wondered if they knew what coffee was. I began to learn that if I showed up somewhere and the hostess offered me coffee, she might be referring to hot water with a powdery brown substance that tastes bad and is not caffeinated to my standards. If you get nothing else from this book, please hear this: instant coffee is not coffee. And I would rather drink the hot water by itself, thank you.

Perhaps it was this misunderstanding and overall blasé attitude toward coffee, along with the many, many comments I received about my frequent Starbucks visits, that drove me to give up caffeine for Lent in Oxford. Rather than wean myself off it and cut one of my three cups a day, I figured I might as well cut all of them out at once.

People have mentioned to me that I can be extreme. Either all in or all out. I've never been able to find that place others talk about so much—the middle ground.

There are other possible reasons I gave up coffee for this particular Lent. At that point in my life, I wanted to be nearer to God, and perhaps subconsciously I felt the need to do some sort of penance to decrease the distance between us. Maybe a severe fast could accomplish this for me.

Or perhaps it was only superficial. I wanted to appear extra holy in my Anglican church or for my atheist friends, one of whom told me, "You know what I'm going to give up for Lent?"

"What?" I asked.

"Lent!" he laughed.

Why I chose to fast from caffeine is not really the point. The point is that I will never do it again. Not for Lent, not for any reason. Barring a serious health concern, coffee will remain my constant. The robotic addiction will be fostered with care. Because coffee is my friend. It is a type of confidant. It makes me feel like life is possible. It makes me happy. It makes mornings worth facing and living richer and more real, and I do not care how sick and junkie this sounds. It is my reality, and I have given myself grace. I have accepted this truth about myself. And now that I know I am capable of living without it—since I did for forty days plus Sundays—why would I ever, ever do it again?

In Oxford I resolved that if I could make it in life without caffeine for forty days, I could do anything. This, as you know, is the purpose of Lent. To test limits. To challenge yourself. To see if you can actually do it. To amaze the people around you with your dedication. This is the purpose of Lent, right? Right?

In the last several years I've noticed the evangelical church adapting more and more High Church practices. They talk about Lent now. At Advent, they light candles and stuff. They might even throw in the occasional response liturgy during a service. This is not how it was for me when I was young and a part of the Church of Christ denomination. We didn't talk about Lent. *That's what the Catholics do,* I thought, *not us.*

This ignorance did not last long. When I was in the sixth grade, I began attending a private school affiliated with the Episcopal Church. I went there throughout middle school and high school, and over the years I received education in the Episcopal Church and its traditions, as well as all the typical required learning in school. We kept them very separate—the church learning and the school learning.

Chapel was held every day at ten o'clock in the morning in a building we called the refectory. Our main chapel service of the year was our Ash Wednesday service, the one that marks the beginning of Lent. Ash Wednesday service was a big deal and about an hour longer than our typical thirty-minute chapels.

I was in the choir, and the choir always performed on this important day. During warm-up, our choir director communicated to us, indirectly, that we needed to be extra good and sing extra well during this particular service. The refectory, which also served as our cafeteria, had windows all around, white tile floors, and a white paneled ceiling. The walls were painted white, and the lunch tables were white. It could be painfully bright in there.

If I squinted my eyes and looked out the windows toward the south, over the interstate and past some hills, I could see the sign for my church. Just behind that sign was the entrance to my neighborhood, where a mile or so of winding road took you up a hill to our house. My entire middle school and high school world took place within a three-mile radius.

The choir sat in the front of the room facing everyone else. This meant we could not get away with talking to our friends, passing notes, or texting. We had to sit, legs crossed, in our formal wear, which was a pleated skirt, button-up shirt, and tie. Even girls had to wear ties.

We also had to sing Kyrie eleison, which means "Lord, have mercy" in Greek, in smooth harmony, with no vibrato—a vocal practice that requires a surprising amount of energy and focus, especially for preteens.

I thought it was the most boring collection of notes ever written, this series of Kyrie eleisons. We practiced it before chapel over and over again, as if significant people would be attending rather than the typical crowd of 350 peers, teachers, and administrators, who often looked just as bored as we were.

"It's not even a song," we complained. "Why do we have to practice it so much?"

It wasn't a song. It was the response in a certain part of the Ash Wednesday liturgy in which our chaplain would signal the entire congregation to sing. But we, as our choir director explained to us each year, were the leaders of this response. We needed to sound good and strong and on key in order to help everyone else sound good, or at least to camouflage the array of sounds school-aged kids make while singing Kyrie eleison.

It went something like this:

CHAPLAIN: God, your love is unconditional.

Us: Forgive our conditions.

CHAPLAIN SINGS: Ky-ri-e-e-le-e-i-son [breath] Ky-ri-e-e-le-e-i-son

WE SING: Ky-ri-e-e-le-e-i-son [breath] Ky-ri-e-e-le-e-i-son

We did some more back-and-forth and then sang again, "Ky-ri-e-e-le-e-i-son." Over and over and over we sang this. To this day I can probably sing it with perfect pitch and no vibrato. Just as I was taught.

At my school, it was cool around the lunch table to talk about what you were going to give up for Lent, and in ninth grade, I did my first Lenten fast: no fried food. Fasting made me feel a little Episcopalian, which at the time felt a little against my religion and church upbringing. I liked this feeling. Participating in Lent made me feel edgy.

But because the refectory served as both chapel and cafeteria, toward the end of the service, smells from the kitchen began to waft in, as if to tease us, saying, "You smell me. I'm a french fry. But you can't eat me. Not for forty days." I always thought holding Ash Wednesday in the refectory was a bit cruel for this reason.

Toward the end of the service, the ashes were distributed among foreheads. This is the part of Ash Wednesday where my evangelical-raised self drew the line. I did the standing and sitting dance of the liturgy. I partook in the Eucharist, dipping my bread in the cup. I recited the Nicene Creed (omitting, in my ignorance and self-righteousness, the part about "the holy *Catholic* church," but that is another story for another time), and I pretended I felt comfortable in all these rituals, like my classmates who had gone through confirmation and been sprinkled as babies. I was the evangelical outsider who was an Episcopalian poser, except when it came to the ashes. The ashes, I could not stomach. They were dirty and I worried what my parents would think if I came home from school with a dark smear on my forehead. So during this part of Ash Wednesday—its namesake, the most important part, the point of it all—I remained seated and looked up at my friends and teachers, who rose in unison and filed into the aisles, ready to go forward and receive the soot in the shape of a cross.

Mr. Lewis was always among the majority who went forward. He was one of our chemistry teachers, and he was completely bald. Because his forehead sort of blended in with the rest of his head, our chaplain always seemed to slightly misplace the ashes, drawing them an inch too high so that he walked back to his seat with a cross nearer to the top of his head than his forehead. I would watch for it each year. I couldn't help it. That bobbing cross, placed so high up compared to everyone else's. Its dark ashen color so stark against Mr. Lewis's light bald skin. It was the most prominent of all the crosses painted that day, hidden by neither hair nor acne. The bobbing cross that walked all over campus on Ash Wednesday.

This is, largely, what Lent was for me in my school years. Singing a single note on repeat, trying to control my breath. Mr. Lewis's bald head. That bobbing cross, made of black ashes, smeared an inch too high.

As you can see, from the start Lent was not holy to me. It was a combination of dreaded chapel services and partial dieting. It was a confusing forty days that lacked true religious implication and consideration of God, Jesus, or the Cross. In fact, Jesus, his death and resurrection, were not central to my version of Lent at all.

Because of these seven school-aged years of confusing and seemingly morally conflicting Lent, still today when my pastor mentions Lent or I read something about it on the Internet as it's approaching, I get a little uncomfortable. I feel a twinge of dread. I feel a twinge of hunger. I feel confusion in my heart and in my head. And to this day, I have never gone forward to receive the ashes.

·❧·

Abstaining from caffeine in Oxford did nothing to reconcile my relationship with Lent. If anything, it intensified uncomfortable memories into February-induced PTSD. A fast from fried food was nothing compared to a fast from caffeine. My other blood.

Mornings, typically my prime hour, felt long and hard without coffee to aid me. My French press stayed in one place on its shelf, and I replaced my morning habit with hot chocolate. It was sweet but did not get the job done the way I needed it done, with a lightning bolt's worth of energy dripping in my veins.

I looked at my bag of coffee beans beside the hot cocoa mix on the shelf in my cupboard, and I am not kidding you, in my decaffeinated state of delusion, Frideswide appeared and mocked me.

"You'll never replace coffee," she taunted in an eerie voice, "but your effort is adorable. Keep it up, saint."

Oh Frideswide. The villain in my tale of an Oxford Lent. This was my battle every morning. Coffee sat on my right shoulder and badgered and badgered me, while the ghost of Saint Frideswide, with her stern narrow face, sat on my left shoulder and told me I was weak and couldn't do it and would never be enough. I had to walk out of the kitchen and retreat to my bedroom simply to find peace and be as far from temptation as possible.

In hindsight, I should have taken my coffee grounds, placed them in an urn, and made a ceremonial march to the Thames before tossing them in. I should have taken a handful, mixed the grounds with water, and smeared them across my forehead in the shape of a cross. For that is what it felt like for me—like sacrifice, like death.

Is what I say here sacrilegious? Quite possibly, but it is the truth. Coffee had died, and I was grieving, the type of grief that didn't quite make it through all the stages. I was stuck in "anger" and never made it to "acceptance."

From February 25 to April 9, 2009, my mitten-clad hands were in a holding rotation of hot cocoa, mint tea with honey, and Diet Sprite. Diet Sprite is gross. Mint tea with honey, though, is not terrible. Even though it looks green and weird and not the color hot water should be, the actual taste is refreshing, and the minty steam reaches deep into your nostrils in a good way.

In spite of the gallons of mint tea I drank during those forty days, giving up coffee did not make me a tea person. I remain suspicious of those who prefer tea over coffee. Have you ever tasted coffee? Do you know its power to transform your entire world?

Lent that year taught me almost nothing spiritually, similar to ninth grade when I gave up fried food, also similar to the next year when I gave up soda. I didn't get it, and honestly I still don't.

But Lent in Oxford did teach me one thing. Though it was accidental and by no effort of my own, it taught me that I like to leave a spoon in my tea.

Through all the hot-drink drinking I did those forty days plus Sundays, I learned how I liked to drink my tea and my hot chocolate. Instead of removing the spoon after stirring in the cocoa mix or the honey or sugar, I found it beneficial to leave the spoon in, so I could keep stirring when the sugar or the mix began to sink to the bottom. I wanted all of the cup's contents to remain mixed. I wanted every beverage consumed at its full sweetness potential. So I kept the spoon clanking in my mug the entire time and stirred and stirred and stirred.

I blame this strange spoon fixation on the abrupt removal of caffeine from my diet. Each recovering addict needs something to draw her attention away from her addiction, right?

By February Jisu had become my most consistent friend in Oxford. The type of friend I could call whenever I wanted without feeling weird about it or overthinking it. Jisu was with me in coffee shops while I worked on school presentations and practiced them for him. We scoured the Internet when I was on the hunt for a new bike. By February we were even discussing taking a trip with another friend to his hometown of Vienna. The fact that someone could actually be born and raised in Vienna was hard for me to understand. Like people who are actually from Paris or New York; I assume everyone there is a tourist.

Our nightly ritual was to lock up our bikes, go into his house or mine, make something warm to drink, and talk, sometimes for hours. Jisu noticed my spoon habit, and he enabled it—the mark of a true friend, I think. Whenever he prepared my drink, he would return to the living room holding both our mugs. His mug with the spoon removed, like a normal person's, and mine with the spoon still in.

He rented a room in a large old home beside the St. Clement's Street bus stop. The house was full of other one-room renters—students, older professionals, internationals—an odd mix. And then there was Jisu, in the middle of them. Young, personable, attractive. Normal.

In my memory, the light in his living room is low, and darkness sits outside the windows. Oxford in winter is dark most of the time.

The sun sets by 4:00 p.m. and rises late in the morning. If you need a good escape from the darkness to some place lighter and warmer, Jisu's living room on St. Clement's Street is a good spot.

Clanking my spoon obnoxiously, I sat on Jisu's couch and complained about the weather and my workload. I had sworn off reading anything for fun. I had time only for books for my classes. This meant day after day I read sad contemporary Irish novels for my Contemporary Irish Literature class and various books about Shakespeare and C. S. Lewis and others I was considering for a thesis. I read heavy literature and drank too much hot chocolate, and all the while I spent lots and lots of time with my Austrian Korean friend. He would talk about his job and his career dreams—Oxford is a good place to dream—and then he would make more tea, and he would put honey in mine and hand me my mug, always with the spoon in. And I would stir and stir, and the stirring lulled me into a type of late-night conversational coma.

With others, I felt insecure clutching my spoon so tightly. But not with him. Not when the dark outside the windows was thick, but the warmth inside was somehow light, somehow thin. Just enough to not smother you and just enough to make you feel safe. It is truly a gift to know another person who radiates that type of heat from his own self.

Who would have predicted an unholy and complaint-ridden Lenten fast would uncover for me a friend who left the spoon in my tea?

·◦∽◦·

There was a deep and dark depth to my disappointment when I arrived at Starbucks Easter Sunday and it was closed. Similar to the sinking feeling we have all experienced when driving up to Chick-fil-A, our mouths watering and ready for some waffle fries, only to remember as our car approaches the drive-through line that it is Sunday.

I had dreamed about it the night before. Coffee. The first cup of coffee after forty days plus Sundays for an addict such as myself is equivalent to seeing the sun for the first time after days of darkness. It's experiencing life again when you thought all life was gone. In a word, resurrection. I had been looking forward to that first cup of Starbucks coffee for what might as well have been forty years, and then, faced with six innocent letters, my dream died.

"CLOSED"

All of Lent crashed before me into a crumbled wall of disappointment.

I should have known. It was 7:30 a.m. on a Sunday. In a small city in England. I should have known, but I didn't, and I stood outside that Starbucks door watching the last forty days play out in an imagined series of animated images reflected in the glass: slow, sad mornings; the resistance to so many temptations; bottle after bottle of diet Sprite; headaches and jitters; that darned Saint Frideswide and her narrow face. Suddenly all of it was for nothing. All of it had meant nothing. Now that my reward was postponed, I could no longer remember why I had fasted those forty days plus Sundays.

Perhaps because I never had a reason to begin with.

7

The Road More Traveled

I think distance can make the heart grow fonder, and distance can make the heart forget reality. Such was the case with my tiny bedroom at the top of the stairs in the house on Donnington Bridge.

The first house I lived in during my time in Oxford, the one before the house on Donnington Bridge, was a sea of beige IKEA furniture on a street called Badgers Walk. My roommates were Americans I knew through some other friends from back home, but they were living there for only a few months on work visas. So by December, it was time for me to make arrangements for a place to live after they left. I scoured church classifieds, the only place I knew to look, for a room for rent, preferably with nice people. A girl named Lizzy had posted about a room in a house farther into town than where I was living. What Lizzy failed to mention was the "room" was actually what I, and most Americans, call a large-ish closet. It was seriously tiny. It had room for one twin bed, one tiny desk, and a matching tiny chair. It had one tiny window on the far wall with a view of the neighbors' gardens and their hanging laundry and no room for clothes or anything other than one's own body.

But I needed a room, and Lizzy and her roommate, Alice, seemed like completely normal Christian English girls, and this house had all the warmth and charm my Badgers Walk home had lacked. No beige here. No IKEA here. It was an old cottage painted white. Wisteria grew over the front door. They had the cutest wooden kitchen table and a real stand-up piano, just like my mom's when I was growing up. Considering these charming elements, the tiny room wasn't so bad. I signed the lease, and soon after, before I moved in my stuff, I went home for Christmas break.

In the weeks I was away, I began to romanticize the quaint British cottage I would return to. I described it to my family as this lovely little place near the river. "My room is the one with the view of everyone's gardens," I said. When I came back to England in January, ready to move into my picturesque cottage with my three enormous suitcases in tow, I was hit with the truth that my heart, due to my time away, had deceived me.

I hauled my bags up the narrow, steep staircase and stood in the doorway of my new bedroom. The room had obviously shrunk since I last saw it. My suitcases did not fit inside it. My own body barely fit inside. I peered out into the hall. A wardrobe sat at the end of it. I had forgotten that because my room was so small, Alice said I could have the hallway too. I could store whatever I needed there or in the wardrobe that sat at the end. A tiny bedroom and a hallway and a wardrobe.

I felt overcome by a wave of claustrophobia. I sank onto my tiny mattress, wondering where all my things would go and how I would manage to live in this space—a closet bedroom and a hallway—for the next nine months. Was everything this size when I came and saw it the first time? Why did I agree to this? I took slow breaths and reminded myself how nice Lizzy and Alice were and how desperately I needed Christian friends. I remembered the stand-up piano in the living room and our cute garden out back.

The wave of claustrophobia subsided and survival instincts kicked in. I could do this. I just needed to be creative with my space. Spaces. I could get baskets for my clothes and use them as drawers, and I could leave my suitcases in the—my—hallway. I could put up curtains and pictures to personalize things. The space issue was nothing but a reminder that I had too much stuff. That all Americans have too much stuff. I did not fit in this country, but as I had been doing for months already, I would squeeze myself in, suck in my gut, put a smile on my face, and move forward. I didn't want Alice and Lizzy to know that I hated my tiny bedroom or that I was worried about where all my wool sweaters would go. I would downplay my American sense of entitlement as best I could.

During my first night in the new room, I almost froze to death. My window didn't shut properly, so the frigid January English air seeped in all night. I woke up several times to the tingling feeling of a different limb going numb. I reached into the night for extra clothes to layer on. By morning I was wearing thermal underwear, flannel pajama pants, a fleece, a sweatshirt and a wool hat with my comforter pulled up to my nose. I was so cold I wondered if I was still alive. "Will I ever even move again? Is this what dying feels like in the Arctic?"

I sat up and eyed the radiator positioned under my window. *A lot of good you did me last night,* I thought. The British, in my opinion, have a different definition of the word *comfortable.* They deal with the cold without coats, and they deal with the rain without umbrellas. They need not keep their radiators on twenty-four hours a day, for that would be wasteful. They keep calm. They carry on. This either makes them superior beings or gluttons for punishment.

The house was quiet that first morning. My new roommates had already left for work, so I was free to snoop. In my wool hat and fuzzy socks, I stepped outside my room and observed my surroundings. I walked downstairs. A built-in bookcase lined the far wall of the living room. I am such a sucker for built-in bookcases. I read the titles of some of the DVDs on the shelf. *Notting Hill, Pride and Prejudice, How to Lose a Guy in 10 Days, Hope Floats.* This gave me hope. This looked just like my DVD collection back home. If we had chick flicks in common, maybe we would have other things in common too.

I left the living room feeling at home. As soon as I walked into the kitchen, I was a foreigner again. I searched the room quickly with my eyes and noticed the absence of many things. No toaster. No dishwasher. No coffeemaker. (No coffeemaker!) And I think that's an oven, but it is very small. There is a washing machine, awkwardly located under the kitchen sink. And no microwave.

That about did me in. In my few months in Oxford, the cultural nuances of England had already left me feeling isolated. The accent, the driving on the opposite side of the road, the weather and constant rain, my clothes, my hair, my teeth. It's not one thing that makes you feel like you don't belong in a foreign country. It is a thousand tiny things that add up before that one thing, and that one thing is simply icing on the cake, the cherry on top, the big straw that breaks the big camel's big back. For me, the straw was living in a house that had a kitchen with no microwave. How would I make oatmeal, sweet potatoes, and popcorn? How would I reheat my coffee?

I sulked back to the living room in my fuzzy socks, feeling completely lost. I sat on the lumpy couch alone and watched the slanting snow outside our window. I realized that watching snow fall when you're alone is one of the loneliest experiences you can have. I didn't like being alone while it snowed. Or I didn't want it to snow while I was alone. Either way, the solitude zapped snow of its magic. And sitting there, alone, while the ugly snow landed on the hard, frozen ground, all I wanted from Oxford was out.

Around the time of the slanting snow, I received an e-mail from my college friend Ashley. "Hey!" it said. "So my roommate is moving out this summer. Wanna come back from Oxford early and live with me??"

Ashley lived in Dallas. This is where most of my friends had migrated after college. I had never wanted to live in Dallas before. I had never thought about it before. But reading Ashley's e-mail at a time like that made Dallas look like an oasis in my desert of winter and foreignness.

Dallas.

It was hot there. Dallas has a mall or two. Ashley had a microwave and a coffeemaker and a dishwasher and a clothes dryer. Her apartment complex had a pool. I could have my own bathroom. I could go to the big megachurch she went to. I could hang out with guys who wore baseball caps and drove trucks and didn't call basketball "netball."

There I was, living in one of the oldest and most renowned cities in the world, and Dallas seemed like the best place I could possibly be. It seemed better than "the city of dreaming spires," as they call Oxford. Dreaming spires looked like crap compared to generic American Dallas. Oh America, how I yearned for it and its highways and roads and gas stations and baseball stadiums and hot weather and red, white, and blue. Right there in the middle of dreamy and beautiful Oxford, I began to daydream about concrete, traffic, and public pools. I began to daydream about Dallas.

Our journeys are much clearer in hindsight, aren't they? When we are out of them and can take a step back and see the full picture, the full map.

I like to think of the uncharted journey as a trail of stones. The stone you stand on right now, today, has a stone in front of it and behind. The stone in front is blurry and covered by thick brush. The stone behind is smooth and shiny, and the step to it is clear. Over and over again as we grow, we have this choice to step onto the stone in front or step back onto the one behind. The way forward is into the unknown. The way back is home, where you came from. And the way back is an entirely feasible option. You can always, always go back. No one will stop you. It is not sinful. It is not wrong to go back. While you journey ahead, in the corner of your eye is the arrow that points home. It's there to comfort you, to remind you where you are from. It's good to have that constant arrow pointing behind you. But just because it's there is no reason to turn around and head that direction. Because you can, doesn't mean you should. But so often we do. So often we take the road back, the road more traveled. I wonder if Robert Frost ever found himself not on a "diverging" road in the wood, but rather, on a straight road, where he looked forward and then back, wondering which direction to go.

We return to what is known for all the sensible reasons we tell ourselves, when really we are only returning because we know what's there. And going someplace you know is so much more comfortable and sensible than going someplace you don't. And I'll say it again, it is not wrong to go back. But let me ask you this, how much faith and trust is required of you when you go home versus when you step into something unknown? Whose knowledge and strength must you depend upon?

You might be standing on a stone that you know, quietly in the back of your soul, requires you to go forward, with a machete, into the brush and fogginess and darkness. If so, the rest of this story is for you. If not, don't worry, you'll find yourself on that stone one day soon, so this is for you too.

Dallas made sense. I had put in my Oxford time. My course ended in September. What would leaving a few months early matter? I could get a teaching job. I could live with my college friend, who lived down the street from our other college friends.

I kept repeating the sense of it to myself: It makes sense to move to Dallas. I should do this. I should go back to Texas. I know Texas. I love Texas. It is so hot in Texas. I would see the sun again. I would remember what it feels like to sweat, to get inside a hot car and feel the leather of the seats nearly burn the skin off the backs of my legs. I wanted that. I wanted hot car-seat leather to burn the backs of my legs.

And so I began crafting My Big Oxford Escape Plan.

I wrote e-mails to people back home. My dad arranged something with a local university's library so I could finish my thesis from Texas. I told Ashley I was definitely interested in the apartment, that I just needed to get some things in order before I gave her the final yes. What *things*? I didn't know, but some ends felt loose and in need of tying.

I told Oxford I was ready to let go of it even if it wasn't ready to let go of me.

I picked a date to leave. June 7. It sounded like a nice departure date. It sounded summery. I told Alice and Lizzy so they could start searching for someone to take my room when I left. I marked it on my mental calendar. I began a mental countdown, tearing off the calendar days happily and with gusto. After a few days though, I didn't tear those pages off so excitedly. I started feeling myself put the brakes on my moving train, but I wasn't sure why.

I went over My Big Oxford Escape Plan in my head. "June 7," I chanted to myself. "I am leaving June 7! I will leave June 7!" The chant, no matter how loudly I chanted it, felt like a lie. I tried harder. I reminded myself that this was what I wanted and this was what I had decided on. Still, unease was rising up inside me. I could feel it. I pushed it back down, trying to remember home and the heat, my college friends, the apartment, the pieces that seemed to fit, but it didn't work. No matter how sensible the sense was that I was trying to make to myself, my insides squirmed around and around and around. Rest did not accompany my sense.

I wasn't able to talk myself into my own plan, and if I couldn't follow my own plan, a different plan must be in the works. For several days I actively did not pray about this. I didn't want to. If God had something else in mind, I didn't want to hear it. Things usually work out well when we actively don't pray about stuff.

One night at church during a worship service, I couldn't take it anymore. Spring was coming, I still had not given a firm answer to Ashley, I still felt restless, and I needed answers. So, forgetting about the whole Lent debacle, I decided to not only start praying about June 7 but to fast about it. Fasting about a date, you ask? I know. I wasn't sure about it either, and it felt a little extreme, but I also felt a little desperate. It was one of those decisions that you decide is the biggest decision of your life and you obsess over it until it is decided.

For the next week, I executed what I call a "dinner fast." Instead of eating dinner, I took a walk somewhere in the city and prayed. It was probably the most prayerfully focused I've ever been about a decision in my life. And it was all about whether to move home in June or stay in Oxford through the summer and possibly longer. It was a season's difference. It was nothing. Yet there I was walking the pastures of Oxford with my dinner (a café mocha) in my hand, asking God about June 7.

Each night of the fast when I got home, I made a big bowl of my favorite British cereal, Crunchy Nut, which I claimed was my "before-bed snack," and went to bed still unclear about my choice.

I recall no grand spiritual revelations during my dinnertime walks, but I do remember one evening walking a trail I hadn't walked before. The sun was still out, and I was beginning to believe there was a possibility that spring did indeed exist in Oxford. Looking to my left I noticed someone had gone before me and taken a detour into the tall grass. I could tell by how the grass was all smooshed in one direction, headed away from the regular footpath. I decided to follow it. I didn't know where this stranger had gone, but I wanted to go there too. The grass and weeds stood tall on either side of me as I followed the flattened grass. After a while, I lost the stranger's trail and had to make my own. The weeds grew even taller now. I thought I must look strange, a girl wandering through the brush away from the trail. I took a few more steps, and then suddenly, without warning, I was right beside the Thames. The grass had been blocking my view, and I didn't realize that the entire time the weeds had been leading me here, to the water's edge.

I stood there for a minute, surprised and delighted to see my good friend, the river. I wondered if God was going to give me an answer about June 7 right here on the riverbank. I wondered if he already had. And then I gave myself permission to stop thinking, to stop praying, and just watch the brown water flow for a minute before returning home.

Later that night, after my bowl of Crunchy Nut, I sat on my bed in my tiny room and determined I was moving back to Texas. I had not heard specifically otherwise, and so that was my decision. I opened my laptop and began e-mailing Ashley to tell her I would be moving into her apartment in June and finishing my thesis from Dallas. I tried to type some sentences, but every combination of words looked and sounded wrong. I started typing again, then quickly deleted. I tried again. Deleted again. *Why can't I word this right? Why does this feel*

so wrong? I kept at it though, typing with uneasy fingers, and finally, after more time than is usually required for crafting a simple e-mail, I finished it. Exhausted, I signed my name at the bottom and hovered my cursor over the Send button.

This is when things got weird. My index finger, the one I use to click my mouse, felt paralyzed. I couldn't click Send. *Click!* I kept telling myself. *Just click it and send! Click!* But I couldn't. My finger remained in a hovering position over my mouse and did not move.

What is happening to me? Why can't I do this? Maybe I just need some rest. That's it. I just need to go to bed and send this in the morning. The fasting, the praying, the walking, it's all made me so tired. I'll do this tomorrow. I'll hit Send in the morning.

So I shut my laptop, put it on the floor, rolled over, and tried to sleep.

All night, I thought about Dallas. I dreamed about it. And in my thoughts and in my dreams, Dallas was dark. Dark, and almost spooky. Dallas in real life is fine. It's just, you know, Dallas. But Dallas in my dreams that night was bad. It was not a place I wanted to live. It was not a place I wanted to be, and at some point in the night, although I did not hear a clear and audible voice from God, I began to feel strongly that my time in Oxford was not over. That the unease I felt with My Big Oxford Escape Plan was because I was trying to force-close a chapter that was not finished being written. I had been feeling uncomfortable in Oxford, and I wanted to feel comfortable and be somewhere familiar again. But deep down I knew that was not a good reason to leave. There were more words to this chapter. I could cut it short if I wanted to, but then I would never know how it ended. I would never know what lay behind the fog and the brush. Sometimes when a chapter isn't finished, it's best not to force its ending.

Of all the feelings, love is the best one. But the second best is that feeling when you know you've taken a step in a scary but right direction. When the path before you is basically covered in trees and the footpath is overgrown and you will need a machete and a lot of courage to uncover it, but you know the path that you cannot see is the best possible path for you to be on. You have this quiet feeling deep down that the path is leading you to the water's edge. It's in these moments—when you choose the half-hidden path in front of you rather than the clear one behind you—that joy and peace hold hands inside your heart. That mix, that joy-peace mix, is rare. When I feel it is when I feel God the most and the deepest. It is my own apologetics. I sit and hug my knees and know he is real because the certainty mixed with the absolute uncertainty and the joy and the peace this produces and their ability to coexist is so otherworldly. There is no way it could have been caused by anything on this earth. There is no way I could have mustered up this peace and joy on my own.

The more I think about this feeling, the more I am able to see that joy and peace are actually products of trust. And not the kind of surface-level, verbal declaration of trust that we Christians are expected to make, but actual trust in a God who we believe is in control and who we believe is good. Trust that we can't shake. Trust that, by his grace I am sure, has slinked its way into our depths so that our entire selves are so confident in who he is and what he is doing that, whether or not we can see his plan clearly, we can feel peace as we take the necessary steps forward. And we can feel joy because we serve a God who is good and loves us and is taking us this way for a reason.

It was such a small thing. Such a tiny decision to decide to stay in Oxford for a few more months. I don't know that it determined my destiny. I think I could have moved to Dallas and been fine. I really do. I don't believe we as humans can thwart God's will with a decision like that. I don't know that it was worth agonizing over, but when I look back at Oxford in the summer, I see it, and I see what I would have missed. I see that trusting God with our unknowns is not always about a dramatic end product. Instead it's much more often about the deepening of a relationship. With each step we take forward into uncharted territory, we face our own weaknesses and, therefore, make space for God's immeasurable strength and care and love. We see, in a way that other circumstances don't allow, that our God, unlike all the other gods, is a God who is truly with us. He is a God who came near and stayed near and will always be near, whether it's time to return home or it's time to move forward.

I never sent that e-mail to Ashley. I didn't open my computer the next morning after the index-finger paralysis. Instead, I stayed put. I let go of Dallas and decided to embrace Oxford, whatever that looked like, whatever would happen.

·❧·

It's funny. The very object that had convinced me I didn't belong in England and needed to move back home was the same object that forced what is to date one of my proudest Oxford achievements: the microwave, or lack thereof. In the end, I conquered life without a microwave. It did not conquer me.

I stood in our small kitchen one day, and I thought about all the people who had survived without microwaves before me. Most people, I thought, most people on this earth and for all of time have been able to make food sans microwave. So could I. And I did, moving from meal to meal. I made oatmeal and popcorn on the stovetop. I *baked* potatoes. I reheated my coffee in a saucepan. It tasted weird and slightly burned, but I adjusted. I adjusted to almost everything in that house. Doing laundry in the kitchen, hanging it on the line outside, watching for rain so I knew when to snatch the laundry back up and move it indoors. Maneuvering a vacuum cleaner they called a *hoover* that looked and acted nothing like a vacuum cleaner.

I collected apples from our apple trees in the backyard. I learned to make things like crumble for dessert (equal parts sugar, butter, and flour) and tomato sauce from scratch. I became hooked on the English version of *The View*, scandalously titled *Loose Women,* that came on at noon every day, and I went to bed with a heating pad at night to help keep me warm. I mastered the French press after watching an instructional YouTube video several times in a row. I hosted people in that little cottage on Donnington Bridge and cooked for them and have never felt so proud. By the end, no microwave seemed like no big deal at all. Home was home and the absence of modern appliances and central heating didn't destroy me or run me out of the country. I even grew to love my closet bedroom with its tiny window and my wardrobe that was awkwardly located in the hallway and was always overflowing with too many coats, too many pairs of boots. I got to know the block, a few neighbors, my local grocery store, the path to the river.

It is satisfying to sit back and realize that what once felt so foreign now feels like a part of you. The people you thought you would never get to know, and even tried to escape from, become friends, and the customs and social nuances you thought would elude you until the end of time begin to piece themselves together. After a little while of patient and careful study, you start to recognize the patterns, then you learn the reasoning behind them, and eventually you love this new place and its strange people. And it doesn't feel so new and they don't seem so strange. You even see a little bit of yourself in them.

Sometimes we must, in faith, simply carry on.

One night in late summer when my departure from England was looming, Alice and Lizzy and I lay side by side on a blanket in the backyard under the stars. I had just accepted a job in Nashville, Tennessee, that started in late September. I would be leaving in the fall, but we weren't thinking about that yet. We were celebrating a job. A real-life adult job. All six eyes looked up at the sky through the limbs of an apple tree. Someone said something funny that sent one of us rolling, and the rest of us laughed at her hysterical laughter. And then, we just kept laughing and laughed and laughed. We laughed and looked up through the tree until the night grew too cool to be outside anymore. I felt so at home there, then, that night. Like that was my place and those were my people. It may have taken me a year to get there, but all of that time, the tears and yearning and questions and homesickness, all of it felt worth it for that one moment and that one burst of laughter.

8

If I Forget You,
O Jerusalem

One day in early February when England was so so cold, I traveled from Oxford to London by car with Jisu, a Canadian, an American, and an Englishman. We sat, knees high, in a too tiny vehicle for the five of us, and I hid my hangover as best I could. I had nearly not come because of this hangover. The night before involved wine, lots of wine, and talking about theology and religion with my friends from school. I had learned by then that wine helped me during nights like these, when I felt out of place, when I couldn't decide if I should be honest about my faith and speak up or simply sit back and watch the conversation unfold. If I was feeling uncomfortable in my own skin, in who I was among these people who were not like me, wine helped. It helped quite a bit. So it had been a night of overconsumption, and I woke up feeling the aftereffects.

Comfortable under my duvet in the early morning light, I formed my cancellation text. "Jisu," it said, "I'm so sorry. I can't go to this Christianity and art conference in London with you today. I just woke up, and I think I might be getting sick ☹" I stared at the unsent text for a long time, still under the covers. I couldn't send it. It was a lie, and Jisu was a friend. I was ashamed of my hangover, and this was a Christian conference. I needed to attend as promised.

I forced myself out of bed and into some warm clothing, and then into some more warm clothing. February in Oxford requires many layers. I paid little attention to my hair or makeup and began the walk downstairs to the kitchen. The walk got slower and slower, and the kitchen got farther and farther away.

Seriously, since when is the kitchen so far from my bedroom? I thought. *Since when did we have so many stairs on our staircase? I will never survive this. I will die on the tenth step if I don't puke everywhere first. Puke. Ugh. Do not think about puking.*

I needed everything: my bed, warmth, a clear head, a settled stomach, energy. Any amount of energy would do.

After lots of tiny steps with long pauses in between, I made it to the kitchen. Coffee was out of the question. Everything edible and drinkable was vomit inducing. I found some butter crackers in the cupboard and forced them down, afraid they would just come right back up. *Stop thinking about puking. Eat the crackers.*

The crackers provided enough relief that I could collect my things and steady myself at the front door. I put on my enormous, full-length, puffy winter coat that probably scared small children who saw me in it from a distance. I was going to this Christian artsy conference thing, hangover and all.

The night before, on my solo drunken walk home, I had slipped on a patch of ice on the sidewalk. It was a very sad and pathetic sight. This morning, in order to avoid a repeat of the night before, I instructed myself to walk slowly and deliberately. There I was. This girl, alone, at seven in the morning on a Saturday, in a coat that could have hidden four other people beneath it, stomping her way along the sidewalk like some sort of clumsy soldier in a sloppy uniform.

If the walk from my bedroom to the kitchen was long, the walk from my house to Jisu's, about one and a half miles, felt like fourteen Mount Everests all lined up and laughing at me. On a better day, I could have run a few miles in that same weather. But on this morning, a mile-long, slow stomping trek made me want to cry and crawl back home.

I dragged my pathetic self inside the nearest corner store. My grandmother taught me that Coca-Cola cures an upset stomach, so I purchased a bottle, feeling a little strange and guilty for using my grandmother's remedy as a hangover cure.

I think, no, I *know* that one bottle of Coke I happened to get my hands on that morning had been prepared by the gods. Some otherworldly, miracle-working creatures gathered the Coke ingredients and sprinkled magic dust on them, then cooked them and bottled them into this glowing thing. This bottle of life-giving, energy-supplying, hangover-curing, and all over feel-good liquid swirled around my organs and brought them back to fully functioning, thriving, blood-pumping, helpful body parts. Just moments before I had become convinced that everything in me was rebelling against everything else in me and my body was waging a war that would end in me collapsing in front of Jisu and his friends in a crying, shameful mess, anything but ready for our Christian conference trip.

I continued walking, clutching my bottle of soda with both mittens, terrified to drop a single ounce of this fairy gold. I had not long to go before I would arrive at Jisu's, and I was feeling more confident with each sip and step that I really would be okay. That I would be able to successfully hide my night-before gulps with a smile and freshness so uncommon for a Saturday morning at seven thirty. Maybe I wouldn't be putting my best foot forward, but I wouldn't be putting my worst foot forward either.

Jisu and the others were standing outside his house on St. Clement's Street when I got there. Everyone had sleepy eyes, and they were rubbing their hands together trying to keep warm. I said hi, and Jisu introduced me to our carpool for the day. A guy from England, his wife from Canada, and another American like me. The five of us squeezed into the English guy's car and made our way to a church in a neighborhood in London I'd never heard of. I wasn't sure where we were headed or what we were headed to. It was a conference. It was about art and its role in the Christian life. It was cheap. This is what I knew.

Everyone was filling out name tags with name and occupation when we got there. "Andrea, Student," I wrote and stuck my name tag on my coat. I looked around at everyone else's. I saw many occupations. Photographer, journalist, artist, writer, painter. I should have made something up other than "student." I felt out of place standing beside the photographers and writers, the people who did real art as their jobs.

I considered peeling my name tag right off when I spotted Jisu waving at me from a row of seats he was saving. I sat beside him, and when he read my name tag, he started laughing. Jisu had written *photographer* on his. Though it wasn't his day job, he was truly talented at it. He had taken me out a few times to try to teach me how to use the fancy camera I had begged my parents for as my twentieth birthday gift, but the lessons didn't stick. Jisu was a wonderful teacher, and I was a hopelessly terrible photography student.

The room was freezing, and I spotted only one tiny radiator in a far corner. I zipped my coat all the way up with a grand gesture. I wanted everyone around me to know that I was not happy with the temperature in the room.

The keynote speaker of the conference was Dr. Gavin McGrath, a pastor and writer. As he began his talk, I tuned in with uncharacteristic attention. I am very good at not listening to sermons and other talks given from stages and podiums. This is a habit I developed as a teen, when the person most often behind the pulpit was my own parent.

But Dr. McGrath was talking about something I had never considered before. Something about truth and art. He said that whatever we do, whatever our art is, as Christians we must be sure it portrays the truth. That is the job of the Christian artist: to tell the truth. This is a biblical concept, not his own. Scripture says it is the truth that sets us free (John 8:32), that we work for the truth (2 Corinthians 13:8), and that we walk in the truth (2 John 1:4). That is our job and our responsibility as Christians who create for a living or for a hobby—to convey truth.

Dr. McGrath then turned to an unexpected passage in Scripture, one I had never paid much attention to before, Psalm 137:4–6:

> How shall we sing the LORD's song
>   in a foreign land?
> If I forget you, O Jerusalem,
>   let my right hand forget its skill!
> Let my tongue stick to the roof of my mouth,
>   if I do not remember you,
> if I do not set Jerusalem
>   above my highest joy! (ESV)

As he read the psalm, I scrambled for my Bible so I could read the passage for myself and underline it. *If I forget you, O Jerusalem . . . If I forget you, O Jerusalem.* I kept repeating the phrase. It felt meaningful, but I didn't know why. It felt like I was receiving a message, but I didn't know what, like someone had just pressed a note into my hand but I wasn't allowed to read it yet.

McGrath told us that these verses from Psalms were written when Judah was taken captive by Babylon. In the verses before, the psalmist explains that the captors were tormenting the Israelites and asking them to sing songs to Zion, to perform sacred worship the Israelites reserved for true worship, not entertainment. This was forbidden. Hence their question, *"How shall we sing the LORD's song in a foreign land?"* Their answer was, simply, to not. And they hung their harps on a tree and remained silent.

Perhaps this is what the Christian artist feels like, McGrath continued. He is in a foreign land, yet he's being asked to perform in the way that all artists are asked to perform. Something in them must create, and there's no stopping it. In the same way, the Israelites knew they must worship God. It was what they were created to do. But how does the artist create when there are scoffers and enemies around, heathens and believers of other religions who may not understand Christians?

Around the time of this conference, my thesis outline was due. I had recently decided to write about a genre called postcolonial literature. It's called postcolonial because it is the literature that comes out of a place and people group once colonized by the West and then left to be independent. Though leaving the colonized nation alone sounds like a good thing, it can cause a time of upheaval. After years of being occupied by these other people, this other culture, the colonized are left floundering in their identity, an identity that has been so defined and wrapped up in their former foreign ruler. The ruler pulls out, and the result is chaotic and painful and confusing. Because of this, things that often happen in the postcolonial novels I've read are bad. Violence, suicide, rape, failure to rise above one's class or escape one's circumstances. The novels have dark themes, and the endings are pretty much never happy. These are sad books. Hard books to read. Tough. Yet, these stories were all I wanted to take off the library's shelves that year. These were the stories I was most drawn to.

This concerned me. I wanted to *want* to write on a more blatantly Christian subject, like C. S. Lewis. I was, after all, living in the hometown of our hero, Lewis. But instead, I kept thinking about these postcolonial stories and themes. They were haunting me. One book in particular wouldn't leave me alone. *The God of Small Things* by Arundhati Roy. I had been assigned to read it in college, and it was so good I packed it up and brought it with me to Oxford. (I like to be in close proximity to my favorite books.)

In *The God of Small Things,* Arundhati Roy wrote one of the most beautifully sad stories I have ever read. It is about love, India and how India was in 1969, the caste system, and sacrifice. Death where death isn't deserved, and life where it's deserved even less.

Velutha is my favorite character and probably the favorite character of everyone who has read the book. Velutha is a tenant worker on the Kochamma family property. He is a Paravan, an "untouchable." He is secretly a part of the communist revolutionary movement, and he is "The God of Small Things. He left no footprints in sand, no ripples in water, no image in mirrors."[5]

And he is in love with the only daughter of the Kochamma family, Ammu. Ammu is a divorcee in danger of being shunned by her family when she returns home after the divorce, her young twins, Rahel and Estha, following behind her like little ducklings.

Before this conference, I had not thought much about the role Christianity played in art or vice versa. Especially when it came to the type of art I was studying, the word type, the literature type. I had always thought it a bit risqué that my professors in undergrad allowed us—students at a conservative Christian college—to read books like *The God of Small Things* or others that spoke of truths we don't normally speak of. I wondered if the entire English department had somehow slid under the radar of the administration's eye. These books felt forbidden. I loved them, but as a Christian, I wondered if I was allowed to love them.

Somewhere along the way I had drawn a line between "regular" art and "Christian" art. I had kept the two neat and separate. There were Christian movies (Kendrick Brothers Productions–type stuff,

---

5. Arundhati Roy, *The God of Small Things* (New York: Harper Perennial, 1998), 250.

certain Hallmark productions maybe), and there were secular movies (everything else). There were Christian novels (by Frank Peretti and Karen Kingsbury, for example), and there were secular novels (everything else). Christian plays, secular plays. Christian paintings, secular paintings. You get the idea. Maybe this is a line you've drawn for yourself too, or maybe this sounds absurd to you. I see now that these labels of "Christian" and "secular" were very weak barriers I had built for myself, barriers based on nothing at all except overt use of the gospel or at least strong and clear metaphors for it. That day at the conference, I saw the weakness and the shallowness of these labels, and so my black-and-white categories, as they typically do with time and age and learning, began to blur.

If we as Christian artists strive to be honest about who we are, like the Israelites in Psalm 137, rather than create something that is Christian, our mission becomes simple: Tell the truth. And if we are telling the truth, then it's no longer a question of whether or not our art is Christian or secular. How can art, a nonliving thing, be Christian or secular anyway? It is not the art that is Christian. It is the artist who *is* a Christian. So instead of asking, Is this Christian or is this secular? maybe we should ask, Is this telling the truth, or is this covering up the truth?

I think you can tell if art is telling the truth by the way it makes you feel. Honest novels, music, paintings, and other types of art invite you to be a part of them instead of holding you at arm's length. When art portrays perfection, you are not a part of it, because you know you are not perfect. You don't see a part of yourself in it. Think about a romance novel or a romantic comedy. The characters are beautiful, chiseled, thin, perfect. Even with their "imperfections," they are endearing—the guy who is too prideful or the girl who is a klutz. Somehow, on screen, they still appear perfectly flawed. I think this type of art is a great escape. When I need to veg and not think about anything, a romantic comedy is my go-to. But in the end, I don't feel like I've necessarily had a cathartic experience. I don't see much of myself in it. The movie, as is the drill for comedies, ends happily. With a bow tied on top, nice and neat. Then I return to my life, my real life, where there are very few bows and, of the few there are, even fewer are nice and neat.

When an artist works hard to portray the less aesthetically beautiful aspects of life, like sadness, loneliness, death, pain, even brutality, I have an opposite experience. I feel like I am a part of the story. Those are the pieces of art that stick with me, haunt me. Like the novel *Crime and Punishment* or the movie *Shakespeare in Love*. I felt the characters' losses. I walked away thinking about the endings for a long time. Both of these works portray life as it is, rather than life as it should be. People end up in prison when they commit murder. A struggling playwright and a rich heiress will never end up together. These types of stories invite me in because I have felt that type of pain and loss too, in my own way and in the universally human kind of way.

You don't come to understand pain or the difficulties of life by painting over them and pretending they aren't there. You come to understand them by admitting they are real and writing them on the page or into the script.

Even though my name tag didn't match anyone else's in the room, I began to feel an inkling of kinship with those around me that day. I began to wonder if they had all already been let in on this little personal and exciting revelation I was having about art and faith. And I began to wonder if maybe it wasn't the darkness of postcolonial literature that drew me to its stories. Maybe what drew me in was their truth and the way the darkness made the truth look so much brighter.

In *The God of Small Things,* you find out soon enough that Ammu loves Velutha back, with a terrifying, absolutely forbidden but absolutely undeniable kind of love. Her twin children love him too.

By the time Rahel and Estha are adults, they are a strange and sad pair. But as young children, they are lively and happy. They see Velutha as the one who helps them build a boat, who plays with them, who is strong. Ammu, the beautiful and practically shunned daughter, falls in love with Velutha for who he is to her and who he is to her children.

Velutha and Ammu begin to meet without others knowing in a house just off the Kochamma family property. Being of different castes, it is against the law for them to love each other. It is something they could be killed for, even in the twentieth century. Velutha threatened "the Love Laws," as Roy calls them, "that lay down who should be loved. And how. And how much."

Each night before Ammu and Velutha leave each other, they make one promise: *"Naaley,"* they say. It means "tomorrow."[6]

Velutha brought Ammu back to life. He gave her a sense of self, and it was a self that she liked. As a single woman and mother in India in the 1960s, she was not welcomed or understood by many, even if her husband had been a terrible man. She was lost. She had moved back home with Rahel and Estha to figure out what to do next, where to go. She didn't even know what her children's last name would be.

Velutha saw the world in the way he could only dream others would someday. A place where caste didn't determine destiny for generations and generations. A place where people were accepted and loved simply because of their humanity and nothing more.

People were against him, though, as they always are with radical thinkers. As the plot builds, you get the feeling that this story will not end in Velutha's favor. Instead, an innocent man will be killed one night while he waits for Ammu to meet him. Someone needed to be blamed for the death of a child, a white child, and it's easy to blame the untouchable, the one who is not only breaking the Love Laws but is, in a way, trying to establish a new law altogether.

A new way that threatened the old.

The police, the ones charged with maintaining order, kill Velutha in the end, and Ammu is trapped in her house, her opposition ignored, her part in it dismissed. Roy describes the policemen's motives: "Feelings of contempt born of inchoate, unacknowledged fear—

6. Roy, *The God of Small Things,* 33, 321.

civilization's fear of nature, men's fear of women, power's fear of powerlessness. Man's subliminal urge to destroy what he could neither subdue nor deify."[7]

·❧·

I ended up reading *The God of Small Things* for my thesis four times. By the fourth read, Velutha and Jesus were basically identical to me. It's not unusual to have a Christlike character in a novel, so I had considered this fact only academically, not personally. But thinking about it later in the context of the conference and art and truth, and the idea that if truth is in art then so is God, I realized something kind of amazing.

Arundhati Roy was not a Christian. I knew this because I had been researching her. Yet she had managed to write one of the most riveting and real portrayals of the gospel I had ever seen. Which made me think, if the gospel can be portrayed by someone who isn't even a Christian, it must be an inescapable story, a thread that runs through everything and everyone.

Over the next few months, as I continued to study Christlike sacrifice in *The God of Small Things* and other novels, I began to see sacrifice everywhere: the changing of the seasons, parents giving things up for their children to have better lives, the crickets who shed their skin in order to grow, the people who do the same. Death is what

7. Roy, *The God of Small Things*, 292.

makes way for life. Every time. We wouldn't have life without it. And as I studied and typed away at my thesis, my concept of Jesus began to form into something very, very real. The faith I had grown wary of and confused about started to articulate itself right in front of me.

I had been looking for God in my church and in my Bible studies. I had expected to encounter him there, but I had not expected to encounter him here, writing my thesis based on heathen-authored novels. As Christian Wiman says, "Art is so often better at theology than theology is."[8]

I learned that I can't limit God's presence in the arts, or anywhere for that matter. Stories of sacrifice, death, and life can't help but reflect Jesus in some way. It's not up to us to decide where he is and where he is not.

If the truth is there, so is he.

The sky had been dark for hours when we got in the car to drive back to Oxford after the conference. Still not warm, I crossed my arms and looked out the window as my fellow passengers talked. Jisu had stayed behind in London with a friend, so it was just the four of us now.

The car debrief began.

"I feel like I'm always disappointed by Christian conferences these days," the American said.

---

8. Christian Wiman, *My Bright Abyss* (New York: Farrar, Straus and Giroux, 2013), 130.

"Oh yeah, why is that?" asked the Englishman.

"The workshops were okay, but they didn't say anything I haven't already heard. And, I don't know, conferences just seem to be lacking something for me."

"I know what you mean," said the Englishman. "I was hoping they would address film more. They hardly spoke about film at all. Film is so central to a conversation about art and culture and faith. I can't believe they missed that."

"What did you think, Andrea?" the American asked. I had remained silent on purpose, hesitant to share my real opinions with people I had just met. I paused for a few seconds.

"Honestly? Besides the fact that it was freezing in that room all day, I loved it."

"Did you?" they asked.

"Yeah, I've never heard Christians talk about art in that way."

"What do you mean?"

"I don't know. I feel like for years I've sort of felt ashamed about the types of books I like to read, the stuff that everyone calls 'sad' and 'depressing.' But being with all of you guys there and hearing what the speakers were saying, I don't know, I feel like the church just gave me permission to like the art that I like."

The car was quiet.

"Hmm, yes," someone finally said.

"Yes, I hadn't thought about it like that," said someone else.

We didn't talk much after that. I returned to my internal dialogue and looked out the window and up at the dark sky. I tried to see the stars, but the city lights were too bright. The farther we got from London, the darker the sky got, and the darker the sky, the more I could see the stars. Something was happening to me, and in me, and I smiled to myself all the way home.

·⟡·

As soon as I got back to my room that night, I scribbled Psalm 137 on a sticky note and stuck it on the wall above my desk.

> How shall we sing the LORD's song
>> in a foreign land?
> If I forget you, O Jerusalem . . .

As I wrote down those words, I started to cry. I was in a foreign land as I wrote about the foreign land. I had forgotten who I was at times. I had dismissed who I was. I had denied who I was. This land was foreign, these people were foreign, and I had even started to look foreign to myself, trying to prove God's existence in my journal, going over the arguments in my head, feeling the expanse that was darkness.

So I wrote the words and I cried and I prayed fervently that I would not forget Jerusalem, that I would hold it above my highest joy.

Maybe the darkness had not been all that bad. Maybe darkness was not about the absence of light but rather about something that forces you to really feel around for things. To really try to grasp them and understand them, to really get to know the world you are in until you can claim it as your own.

The hangover from early in the morning had worn off now, and after months of feeling around for my faith, I finally felt a welling up inside me. A welling up of what, I wasn't sure. But it felt honest and truthful and bubbly. It felt like an old desire that had never quite left and was returning to me, and it looked like the light from a hallway that squeezes through the cracks into a dark room, just before the door is pushed wide open.

9

English Gardens

I spent a lot of time in a wild garden behind a house in east Oxford. I had taken an internship with a publisher in town. The publishing house turned out to be a shed in his backyard. It was a start-up specializing in travel books, his passion project. Two afternoons a week I would ride my bike up the hill to the house where he and his family lived, walk through the front door, through the kitchen, out the back door, and through the garden to the shed. The publisher sat at a desk on one side, and I sat at a desk on the other. One of his authors was writing a book about the Danube, Europe's second largest river. This author didn't like computers, so he typed his manuscript and mailed us the pages. It was my job to type them into a Word document. I learned more about the Danube than I ever cared to learn.

I loved the garden that surrounded that little shed. My boss and his wife grew all kinds of things back there: tomatoes, zucchini, beans. There were hydrangeas and, since hydrangea is one of the only flower names I know, let's just say there were lots of other flowers back there too. I house-sat for them once, and each day I sat on their back porch, looking at the garden while I ate breakfast.

The English know how to garden. If you have a front yard in England, you don't let it go untended. It seemed everyone had a garden, and each one was beautiful in its own wild way. They were not obsessively groomed. Bushes poked out from behind fences, and flowers were planted close to each other, so when they grew their colors overlapped. Vines were set free to grow tall and bend over onto the footpath. They were not trimmed or considered a nuisance. The English gardens I saw and noticed were overcrowded and out of control and unpredictable, and in this, they were free. Beautiful and free.

The road connecting South and West Texas—Highway 84, 83, or 283, depending on where you are—is long, flat, and straight, but it leads you into the most vivid sunsets you will ever see. Because there are no hills or trees to block the view, sunsets in West Texas can be replicated nowhere else on earth. Of this I am sure. Before the sun sets, what you have to look at is sparse. Dead grass in summer; dead grass in winter. Tiny oil rigs in the distance, and flat-roofed ranch houses, houses that are home to kind, Texas-in-their-blood types of families. This is the land my father grew up in, the land where I visited my grandmother when I was a child, and the land where I attended college.

The drive looked the same all the dozens of times I made it. The familiar succession of cities: Coleman, Santa Anna, Brady, Mason, and Fredericksburg. All towns that look like what you think of when you think small Texas town. Depending on which way you are going—toward Abilene or away from it—they grow or get smaller in size.

On this trip toward the big city of San Antonio and away from Abilene, I rode with my friend Ashley. We were going to be volunteers for a youth group retreat at my church, and as we drove the Beast We Needed to Talk About sat on the console between us.

Ashley was one of the first girls I met freshman year. I remember her standing in the doorway of her room. She had auburn hair—real, natural auburn hair, the type you don't see very often. We were going to be friends; I knew it right away. Ashley was enthusiastic about all things college. She was enthusiastic about the dorm, about being a freshman, and especially about finding our future spouses at Abilene Christian University, so we could all have ACU-bound babies together. She endeared herself to all of us with her energy and the way she told stories. Her thin arms sort of flailing about and her hair in a ponytail up high on her head. She was our lanky, fun, auburn-haired friend.

Perhaps I wasn't the only one who felt this way about Ashley, but when we sat together and talked, I felt our spirits link up. She got me, and I sort of got her. Ashley and I were friends, good friends. I had a confidence with her.

By our sophomore year, though, right before our road trip from Abilene to San Antonio, I began to wonder if Ashley was okay. She was not as enthusiastic or energetic. She didn't come around as often. I didn't meet up with her for lunch after chapel the way I used to, and I noticed something else. She was getting thin. I didn't think much about it at first because she had always been thin, but one night in my friend Laura's dorm room, I got the feeling something was off.

"So Ashley thinks she can't eat with us in the cafeteria anymore," Laura said.

I looked at Ashley. "What? Why? I know you haven't been eating with us, but I thought that was just because you like being by yourself sometimes."

"No," interjected Laura, "the other day she told me—"

"Excuse me. I'm sitting right here," said Ashley. "We don't have to talk about this right now, okay?"

"Fine," Laura said.

"Okay," I said. And we quickly changed the subject.

The whole exchange was a little unsettling. Ashley looked upset. I had not thought to question her motive for always eating alone, for never coming to the cafeteria with us, for always having excuses to not eat out at restaurants. Ashley was independent. But this was college. And in college even we independent types don't like eating alone when a cafeteria full of our friends is nearby.

I had been thinking a lot about that dorm room conversation, and now, on this particular road trip from West to South Texas, it was What We Needed to Talk About.

We passed through the tiny no-name towns of populations like 132. We looked out the windshield at miles of earth that was cracked and dry and had always been that way. Lifeless fields. I'm sure we talked like we normally did, about boys and friends and school—and boys. Each lull in the conversation a reminder of what we weren't saying.

There is something about a car, isn't there? And a road trip? And the no-escape feel of it all? The person in the seat beside you is your captive audience or you are theirs. And where there is something unspoken between the two of you that has been hovering for a few days or weeks or even just hours, it will now sit between you for the duration of your journey. You can't glance at the other person without seeing it—the thing you need to say, the question you need to ask. When you talk about anything other than the thing, you will have to yell over it or around it until you give up and say nothing at all. Until one of you stumbles upon a brave moment and addresses the sitting Beast between you. The moment you do, it disappears so you can see each other again.

I was no expert in eating disorders. I wasn't even willing to speak the phrase aloud. It sounded so . . . disease-like. I didn't even know if that was what she had. I didn't know the warning signs. I certainly wasn't the most qualified person to speak to her that day, but I was a friend, and I couldn't ignore the evidence. Not eating meals with us, being distant, and of course the evidence her body itself provided. It was beginning to disappear. Little by little, a centimeter here, an inch there. Ashley had shrunk, and maybe that's what she wanted. Maybe she wanted to shrink until she disappeared. And if that was true, how do you tell someone to stop disappearing when she is doing all she can to fade away with as few people noticing as possible? Like we would all just look up one day and—no Ashley.

So as we drove along the highway, I knew if I was going to be a good friend to Ashley, like she had been to me, I couldn't let something like this go. Good friends don't let you get away with potentially self-destructive behaviors. Good friends sometimes have to be my least favorite word, *confrontational*.

"So, what Laura said the other night in the dorm, what was that about?"

"Oh nothing. I said something the other day about food or whatever and . . . I think she just didn't get what I was saying."

"Hmm. Okay, yeah." I was quiet for a minute. "Well, I have noticed that you don't eat with us anymore."

"Yeah."

"And I have noticed that you've lost weight this year."

Ashley was quiet.

"Do those things have anything to do with each other? Maybe?"

"I don't know. I mean, yeah. Probably. I have lost weight. You're right about that."

I looked over at my friend from the driver's seat. She looked so small, snappable. And even though she was sitting right there, she looked far away. I wanted to pull her back, but not too hard.

We drove along on the dry road ahead, and we talked for a good long time. Ashley began to explain something to me that, even though I hadn't gone through what she was going through, made sense somehow.

"It's kind of become a game for me," she said. "I weigh myself at the same time every day. If I've lost weight, I get a point. If I haven't, I don't get a point. I don't go out to eat with y'all because I'm afraid to. I'm afraid eating regular food would make me gain weight. I don't want to gain weight, and I feel like if I go with you, I'll gain four pounds. I know that sounds crazy, but it's how I feel."

We drove through yet another tiny town and down the barren road that would take us to the next one.

At some point Ashley cried, and at some point I began to pray while driving, with my eyes open. I don't remember my words, but I'm sure they were clumsy. I wonder if they fell empty onto her lap. If what she was facing was still at such an early stage that praying for "freedom" from it was premature? The first step toward freedom is wanting it. I wonder if she simply stared out the window on her side as we passed through Brady and turned right at the furniture store with the giant carved-wood bears out front. The land got drier and drier, and we saw no trees.

Later, Ashley told me that our conversation in the car that day was the first time she had articulated aloud what she was going through. Until then, it was this very private game. Now I knew, and soon others would know. She would tell her family. She would tell other friends. She would tell a counselor. It didn't happen at once in the car that day, but Ashley's fears and entrapment in the game eventually began to let go of her, or she let go of it. She started a new path, a new way, a greener one, and we were all so thrilled when Ashley, the Ashley I had met freshman year in the dorm, began to come back to us. When she started eating with us again and being with us again.

I didn't gain the "freshman fifteen," but my "junior study-abroad fifteen"? It was something to behold. Add to that a "heartbreak fifteen" due to the recent breakup—the one that had sent me wandering the streets of Oxford alone, listening to Coldplay on my iPod—and an entirely new wardrobe was in order.

I gained the weight happily at first. I was traveling with friends on the weekends—to places like Italy, where I ate cheese and bread, and to France, where I drank hot chocolate and ate crème brûlée as my afternoon snack. In England we ate late-night sandwiches and large bowls of chocolate granola before bed. I didn't know I was eating my feelings. I didn't really know what eating your feelings meant.

But then I returned home at the end of the semester and reached into my drawer for a pair of pants I had left behind. I pulled them on, and the pants would not button. A few months earlier this pair of pants was loose, almost too big. Someone had shrunk them. My mom must have dried them while I was away instead of hang-drying them. The possibility I had grown a full pants size over the course of a semester didn't cross my mind. It took several pairs of pants before I agreed to even consider what had happened. That, while the chocolate granola I devoured in England was not available in US grocery stores, I had brought some of it home with me, permanently.

That summer my family loaded the suburban to drive the road to West Texas, this time to say good-bye to my dad's mother, Thelma. I sat in the middle of the backseat, between my sisters, me and my extra fifteen-plus pounds, and I stared at the dry, familiar earth ahead. I devised a plan for myself right then and there on the way to my grandmother's funeral. I was going to lose the weight I had gained and then some. No matter what it took, I was going to lose it.

On the way there, we stopped at a small Subway restaurant in a gas station. *My first test,* I thought. I ate only half my sandwich and put the other half away. I smiled to myself when I realized what I had done. I had dug deep and found an ounce of self-control. I didn't know I had that—self-control. I had always had a strange relationship with food and my body. I ate what I wanted when I wanted, but then I would feel guilty, so I'd exercise. I began exercising regularly at age fifteen. I knew exercise. It wasn't a problem for me. But food? That was different. And how I saw myself in the mirror? That was bad. I wasn't overweight, but I was never the weight I wanted to be. Even at a young age, I remember wishing I was thinner. Always thinner. Just a few more pounds. But I didn't think I had it in me to lose weight. I didn't know how. Food had always felt like a power beyond me, too great for me. That's why eating half my sandwich at the gas station that day felt like a miracle. I had tapped into whatever it was that other skinny people had tapped into. And with the strongest grip I could muster, I held on tight.

The Lucados met up in a hotel lobby in Andrews, Texas, where my dad had grown up and where my grandmother would be buried the next day. Then we caravanned to the nearest Mexican restaurant. We were there to catch up, share stories of grandmother, to be together. But I was not with them. Externally, I was having conversations with my cousins, but in my head was a stressful dialogue and debate.

How many chips should I eat? How much cheese would be on this taco versus this salad? If I got dressing on the side that would help, and avocados are good for you, but they have a lot of calories, right? And the Mexican rice, I wonder if that's cooked in oil. Is it better to balance out the carbs in the chips with extra beans instead of rice? Oh, but the beans are cooked in lard? No. Off. Limits. Dessert is certainly out of the question, and so is Coke. But Diet Coke—I could drink that because the bubbles will make my stomach feel like it's full and then I won't want to eat as many chips.

It sounds insane, especially written out on the page like this, these incessant thoughts that occur over a simple decision on a menu. But I've heard of people having panic attacks from looking at restaurant menus. It happens.

I lived in this insanity all summer until it became my normal. I showed up at school that fall semester a smaller person and proud of it. I had learned to restrict my eating. My motto? EAT NOTHING YOU WILL REGRET LATER. And I stuck to it. Instead of eating until I was full, I ate until I was almost satisfied. If midbite I realized I was satisfied enough, I spit it out. I actually spit food out of my mouth. Sometimes I threw it away when no one was looking. I remember being outside with my family one night, looking at the stars. Everyone was eating these really delicious cranberry, white-chocolate-chip cookies. I ate half of mine and felt so guilty, I threw the other half in the bushes. My sister saw me.

"What are you doing? I would have eaten that!" she said.

My senior year of college, I thought about food and exercise most of the time. Sometimes I felt dizzy when I stood up, and sitting too long hurt my backside.

I didn't look like I had an eating disorder. I looked great, actually. Better than I've ever looked in my life. I began to like pictures of myself instead of cringing at them. I felt so victorious and in control of everything, not just my diet but my entire life. I felt like I had conquered food, something I thought I could never control. Though my body mass index would not have alarmed any doctors, my head, my heart, and my soul were trapped. It was a new type of bondage. The most dangerous type. The type you don't even know you're in when you're in it and, therefore, make no attempts to escape.

At school, I received compliments from others and comments about how great I looked. "You've lost weight!" I remember one friend saying after seeing me for the first time that fall.

"I have!" I said and smiled. One point for me.

I received compliments from everyone. Everyone but Ashley. Ashley had remained strangely quiet about the new me. This was irritating. All my friends had recognized my weight loss and thought I looked good, but Ashley didn't address it. Not at all, not until the day we found ourselves on another road trip, on the very same road as before. This time in Ashley's car with her in the driver's seat and the Beast Between Us being my own weight.

We were on our way back to school from Austin, where a group of us had traveled together for the weekend. By no accident at all, I ended up in Ashley's car on the way home. I stared out the window this time, proud of my accomplishment, wanting my friend's—this particular friend's—approval and not receiving it. We passed Brady and Coleman and Santa Anna. I saw the landmarks I could have seen in my sleep. The sun was not near setting, and it lit the road ahead as it cut through the dryness.

I decided to bring it up myself if she wasn't going to.

"So I lost a lot of weight this summer," I said.

"I know. I've noticed."

"You have?" I looked over at her in the driver's seat. "You haven't said anything about it. I've been wondering why you haven't said anything." It felt foolish to ask for affirmation, but I needed it.

Ashley still didn't compliment me, but she did begin to ask questions.

"Has it been hard for you to do simple things?"

"Um, no, not really—"

"What are your thoughts like? Do you think about food a lot? Calories?"

"Well, sometimes, I guess—"

"Do you still have your period?"

"Yes! I'm not *that* skinny."

"Well, I don't know. You lost a lot of weight and fast too. That can happen."

I didn't like this conversation. I wanted her to be impressed, like the others around me. Somehow I had completely forgotten our exchange in the car a year and a half ago. Somehow my weight loss was right while hers had been wrong.

Ashley told me some hard things that day. The things she had worked through since the tables were turned. Things I didn't want to hear about, like freedom and reason and health. She told me about a book her counselor had given her.

"You should read it. I'll make photocopies for you."

"Okay," I said. But I didn't want the photocopies. I didn't want to read that book. I didn't want my newly found sense of control to go away. I was afraid if I let go of my new healthy habits, everything, not just my weight, would fall apart.

I ignored Ashley's words that echoed in my head loudly, and I ignored them for as long as I could. In the car that day with the road endless ahead of us, freedom seemed a long way off. It would take a year or so, and it would take another stint in the British land of lushness and rain and gardens that grew free.

·⌒·

One of the most surprising differences between me and my female English peers was physical appearance. To me, at the time, American women had one look, or one desirable look: thin and put together. We had straight teeth. We exercised in order to be certain shapes, to have certain lines. We had flatirons and curling irons and things to tame our hair when it got unruly. Our clothes were pressed and matched fairly well. We were neat, ironed, big-smiled, exercising Americans. We did these things because of the standard of beauty in which we were raised. I knew what it took in America, and specifically in Texas, to be considered pretty. And the look was neat, streamlined, controlled.

English girls were so different from us. At first I thought there were no trends or standards in England at all. They all seemed to wear whatever they wanted, whenever, and I couldn't keep up. After a few weeks, though, I noticed some commonalities: big scarves, dresses and tights—no matter how cold or rainy it was—worn-in shoes or boots. Nothing looked new or perfectly ironed or pressed. Clothes looked as if they had been crinkled in the back of a drawer for years. I didn't see as many English girls running like I did. Many of them wore less makeup too, or none at all, and they didn't seem concerned with their hair when the rain and humidity turned it wavy and out of control. Instead of chastising it by pulling it back into a ponytail, they let it fall freely on their shoulders, untamed.

I sensed a freedom in British women and grew thirsty for it. I thought they were delightfully different in the way they dressed and the way they ate and talked, or didn't talk, about their bodies. I watched how they were. A part of me watched out of cultural curiosity. How *do* the English live? But a part of me watched as a girl who felt trapped by rules and ideals, a girl who secretly wanted out.

Some of my English friends were wonderful cooks. They made spaghetti bolognese and baked chicken and vegetables on Sundays. They ate bread and carbs in all forms without whining and saying, "Ugh, I really should cut back on my carbs." They enjoyed good food, which was a very novel idea for me at the time.

They didn't seem to obsess over their outfits or dress size. They didn't fuss over their hair and makeup. They were a natural and relaxed I'm-going-to-cycle-to-this-party-even-though-it's-raining-outside-and-my-hair-will-be-a-mess-by-the-time-I-get-there species, and I observed them as an objective anthropologist. In their natural habitat, they showed me, even though they didn't know they were showing me, how other women lived in another part of the world. And I took notes furiously.

I remember the turning point for me. It was during a weeknight church meeting at St. Aldate's. Weeknight church meetings often included a meal cooked by the resident chef. On this night he served banoffee pie for dessert. Banoffee pie is an English dessert done right. Condensed milk and banana and toffee—hence "banoffee"—on piecrust, and maybe some whipped cream on top. And maybe chocolate drizzled on top too. There aren't many foods I discovered in England that I wish were more prominent in the States, but this is one of them.

I looked at the pie on the plate in front of me. I lifted my fork, and then I did something that a year before I would have never done. I ate the entire thing. Every grain of sugar. Each grain of all-purpose flour. Each ounce of butter. Each drop of condensed milk and each crunchy bite of toffee. I scraped up what was left on the plate with my finger and licked it off. I kept telling myself to have only one bite or to eat only half of it, or only three-quarters of it, but I couldn't stop. I wanted all of it, and when I put down my fork, I realized something important: I was okay. I didn't feel a panic attack coming on. I didn't feel overwhelmed by guilt or the need to go run six miles. I looked up from my empty plate and saw that the self-control I had been so proud of had been melting away over here in England without my even realizing it. And that was a very good thing for me.

Not all at once, of course, but by the end of that year in Oxford, I didn't think about food in the morning and at night anymore. I didn't restrict my calories, and I hadn't told myself EAT NOTHING YOU WILL REGRET LATER in a very long time. I ate what everyone else did. I ate banoffee pie and other desserts without sweating or experiencing chest pains. The internal dialogue typically caused by restaurant menus changed from *What would be the least damaging?* to *What sounds best to me right now?* None of it was intentional. I arrived in England still not fully aware of my issues with food, but something happened being around these people who were not desperate to control their surroundings, who shrugged their shoulders at the consecutive rainy days and mounted their bikes anyway. Who didn't care that they showed up with rosy cheeks and windblown hair or that their boots would get muddy as they walked along the river. Who didn't have to use a flat-iron every single day or match their outfits perfectly. Who ate carbs and real food and didn't bring up their diets in every conversation. Whose gardens weren't groomed to perfection and who allowed their plants to grow wild and tall and poke out from behind fences. These people who just seemed to be able to let go and enjoy more. All of them, all of it, the wildness of the English countryside, the attention to the good, slow, and simple parts of life, the overall healthy attitude created this incubator for me that year. A safe place in which I could release a big, deep sigh.

IO

River Conversations

What is it about my running shoes and my feet hitting the pavement in a familiar pattern that gives my mind permission to wander so? My body is at home in the rhythm, and my brain is free to think of nothing practical or present. It wanders back and it wanders forward. It takes the beginning of an ache in my hips to pull me into the moment, as only pain can do.

On a Sunday morning, just after the fog lifts, I leave my house in a T-shirt, a pair of running shorts I've owned for too many years, and my neon-green Mizunos, not knowing how far I will go this time. I head away from downtown Nashville, where I live, to an unknown destination.

I'm thinking of Jisu while I run because it's a safe place to dwell on him for a minute, to think about what he's doing now and how he is. On this foggy morning, Jisu is a friend who lives in the haze of what-could-have-been. An almost kiss. A late night at the kebob truck. A bike ride with a headlamp on. Coffees, teas, pizza, and noodles.

My mind runs to him and wonders.

We spent the day together in London once. It was during our fuzzy time. Are we friends? People think we're dating, so are we?

The day in London was going well. We had caught an early bus and eaten croissants on the ride. We toured the National Gallery museum. We lifted our heads up in unison to stare at St. Paul's Cathedral. He indulged my craving for a McDonald's ice-cream cone.

Yes, everything was going well, until the Tate.

The Tate Modern is a large gallery of modern art, better appreciated by those who can understand the artistic value of an apple balancing on a stool or a ladder leaning against a wall, leading to nowhere. But it is very famous and, therefore, made its way onto our To Do in London list.

Separating us from the Tate Modern was the Millennium Bridge, an impressive and expansive piece of architecture that crosses a very wide part of the Thames. Jisu and I happily began the trek across, but by the time we reached the other side, my mood had changed.

Art museums are romantic. Maybe not to everyone, but they are to me. Taking in art is an intimate experience, and to be at a gallery with a man who was not my boyfriend but not exactly just my friend made me not know how to act. I didn't want to be looking at different paintings in the same room, dispersing from each other and occasionally coming back together, only to brush shoulders and part again. I wanted to do the Tate together, holding hands as he led me around and we pulled each other in different directions to view different displays, side by side. Not as distant friends separated by a heavy question mark.

After the Tate we ate at a burger place.

"Are you okay?" Jisu asked me from across the table.

"Yeah, I'm fine. Why?"

"You are being, I don't know, quiet."

"I'm just tired."

"Oh, okay."

On the bus ride home, he asked again.

"So nothing is wrong? You are fine?"

"Yeah, really. I'm tired. I think I'm gonna try to sleep." I leaned my head back and closed my eyes. I kept them closed the entire ride, but I never actually fell asleep. I only pretended to. I stayed like that until I felt the bus break at our stop on St. Clement's Street in Oxford. I followed Jisu off, both of us sluggish from a full day of tourism. He lightly hugged me good-bye, and I said, "See you soon," because Jisu and I always saw each other soon.

Not long after the Tate, Jisu and I talked. He came over on a Sunday afternoon before the evening church service so we could walk there together, the long way. The river way. I was always up for a walk along the river, but I knew this one could get clumsy. I didn't want to talk to Jisu because I knew we needed to discuss serious things about being friends and being something more than that. "Friends" did not stay up so late sitting on the couch with their arms pressed up against each other. The word *friends* had been slowly, and not surprisingly, disappearing from the types of words that could define our relationship. And now, we were taking the long way to church.

I focused on the river at first. I was good at that. That particular part of the river nearest to my house had grown so familiar to me by now. The path beside it was muddy always, whether it had rained that day or not. My favorite part was where the trail gave way to the cow pastures and I ran on the uneven grass, feeling like I was trespassing. But in England, running on someone else's cow pasture is not trespassing. They share land there. It's a wonderful thought, so polite.

And so we walked and talked a little about our days, and I looked into the water.

"I didn't wear a warm enough jacket," I said.

"Yeah, it is still very cold for springtime. You never seem to wear a warm enough jacket though," he joked.

"I know, but look, I'm wearing two pairs of leggings, and I'm still cold!"

"Maybe we should not have walked beside the river. It is always colder here. Do you want to cut over to the street?"

"No, no this is fine. I love the river. Let's just keep going this way."

I liked Jisu. One recent night on my couch while we hovered over his laptop looking at something, I really wanted him to kiss me. I really wanted to be his girlfriend, and I really wanted him to hold my hand. But I also felt like I was in a state of limbo with him that I couldn't escape, like a boat on the river that couldn't quite make the dock.

We neared the houseboats that had aligned themselves as a neighborhood—the official guardians of that section of the Thames. We chose a bench near this makeshift neighborhood of houseboats and sat down to begin the real part of our conversation. We did not sit close to each other. The question mark had wedged its way back between us now.

"So," he began, "friends have mentioned to me that they've noticed we're spending a lot of time together."

"Yeah, we have been. I know how that starts to look to other people. My friends have been wondering too."

Jisu and I looked at the river. Back at each other. Back at the river. The water was brown, but not in a murky way, and the leaves, which had recently returned to the limbs of trees everywhere in Oxford, swept low and back and forth, threatening to break the surface of the water but just missing it each time. Around our feet small white flowers had begun to grow out of foliage recently freed from hibernation. It didn't feel like spring in this part of the world, but it definitely looked like it.

"I have come to really respect you," Jisu said, "and I enjoy spending time with you. I think you know how I am feeling?"

I looked at the river and those leaves, wondering if they would get swept up by the current this time.

"Yes," I said. "I think I do know how you feel, but we haven't really talked about it before, you know?"

"I know. But I feel the need for this conversation now. Maybe it is finally time to talk about it."

I didn't say anything. I was scanning my thoughts waiting for the exact right combination of words to reveal themselves to me.

"I just don't know how I feel," I finally said. "I know I like being friends with you. Like the other night, when we were sitting on my couch."

"Yeah," Jisu said, knowingly.

"But, right now, I don't know. I'm just not sure. Is it okay to not be sure?" I looked down. Jisu's hand gripped the edge of the bench several inches from mine. The houseboats bobbed. We sat. Both of us still, afraid to move. Afraid of disturbing whatever it was we had.

Behind our bench lay Christ Church college. Its buildings glowed more and more yellow as the sun slid lower and lower. Separating us from the campus was a long meadow bordered by a tree-lined path. The most perfect of places to say "I love you" was under those trees. To hold hands for the first time. To kiss. Nowhere else in Oxford would have been more perfect.

"It's okay to not be sure," Jisu said finally. We turned toward each other.

And that was when the Thames paused. It stopped rippling and turned and looked at us. It gave us the window of a moment to kiss and declare deeper feelings. It waited for a good long time, but eventually when it realized that wouldn't be happening, it rippled on again and flowed quickly to catch up with itself.

·❀·

As much as I love the question *why?*, there comes a time to stop asking it. When *why?* turns into *what if . . .* , I know I've been dwelling on the same story for too long and it's time to let go of the situation, whatever letting go of the situation looks like for that particular situation, and move on, whatever moving on looks like. I have given too much backward attention to these types of conversations. The ones in which I feel like the river gave me an opportunity and I passed it up. I think about them when I am running and when I lie in bed trying to sleep. Sometimes I dream about them and wake up confused. Conversations that occur by the river will make you crazy, if you let them.

River conversations are river conversations because they have so many options and directions. They twist. There are tributaries. There are shallow parts and deep parts. There are obstacles and people living in houses on the water, people walking beside the water—so many distractions. River conversations could have led this way and that, so it's no wonder we can't stop thinking about the options. A simple yes would have taken us there. A simple no? Somewhere completely different. You've said no and wished you said yes. You've said yes and wished you said no. One thing rivers don't do is switch directions. They don't flow backward to a place they've already visited. They go one way, so those river conversations in your head, though you wrestle through and wonder about all the options, you will not, in reality, be given another opportunity to select one of those options. There are no truer words than *What's done is done*. It is. It really, really is.

A friend in Nashville once told me that when he hears conflicting and confusing voices in his head, he knows those voices are not from God. God is not a God of confusion, he explained to me. God is clear. When I regret, wonder, and question my past, I feel anxious, guilty, and foggy. But when I release those moments of opportunity offered by various rivers over the years, and I focus on what's in front of me and all around me, the fog clears, the guilt fades, the anxiety subsides. That's when I hear God's voice because I've finally quieted the others. That's when I can see his face. Through the clearing of the fog, he comes into view, and his eyes are kind.

Maybe today, years later, the Thames would witness a different story. Maybe it wouldn't be a patch of river that twinges a little with disappointment when it thinks of that conversation between me and Jisu. Or maybe it knows, maybe the river always knows how it is going to end. Maybe it understands better than we that sometimes our spirits say no to other spirits without ever fully understanding why.

I'm still running, but the pain in my hips snaps my thoughts back to the present. I've already run a few miles, and now I am making the turn into Centennial Park, Nashville's iconic park. In the middle of the park sits a full-scale replica of the Parthenon in Athens. On the lawn in front of the Parthenon, people are usually playing flag football or ultimate Frisbee. I don't often go to Centennial Park because it beckons the image of this giant, somewhat out of place, pillared beast of a building. I forget about the part behind the building. The beautiful part with a large pond, trees that shade the path, and light that reflects off the water and seeps through the trees in such a way that, even as I run by, I turn my head just to keep watching it. The light. I loop the park for a double take.

I pass many other runners on the trail, smarter ones who thought to wear gloves on the first cold morning of fall. I blow on my numb fingertips and wonder if the other runners are also breathing in Centennial Park today as I am. Is it just me or did this place suddenly get so lush? Has the light always fallen on the water like that? And I think as I round the path away from the pond that every part of this is truly a gift.

People have said that to me before. "Life is a gift, Andrea, and everything in it. A gift from God." I pretend I understand them and nod my head in agreement. What am I going to say? What I'm really thinking? That things are not gifts if they are for everyone. Gifts are supposed to be for individuals. They are tailored to the receiver, picked out depending on preference, and then wrapped for one, *one* person to unwrap. To say life, or parts and aspects of it, is a gift, well, that didn't feel special enough or unique enough to me.

But this morning in Centennial Park, unable to turn away from the light on the water, I feel the gift. It feels only for me, and maybe for the first time. There are others around, and though they aren't craning their necks in the opposite direction of their feet like I am, they are noticing the light too, and they see that the wind moves the trees in a way that could lull you to sleep. They see that ducks are not sitting on the water; they are floating so delicately it is more of a hover so as not to disturb the pond beneath. They form no ripple. And everything is alive in the screenshot, living breath in each direction. How have I not noticed before? And it is this consciousness that is the gift, not necessarily the light, water, and trees themselves, but the connection they are making with my eyes, my brain, my heart. I feel their life and am aware of their beauty. Unwrapped and somehow only for me.

Back on our bench, Jisu checked the time on his watch. It was almost time for church. We stood up together, having resolved very little. We walked past the meadow, along the tree-lined path. We kept our eyes forward and space between us. The sun set behind Christ Church, and our shadows stretched long.

11

The 0.1-Mile Pilgrimage

August thawed Oxford. It came in and subdued the cold in a way no other month had been able to do. Bodies emerged from everywhere. Bare arms and legs swinging about, pale and grateful.

Summer, in general, is my favorite. But summer in Oxford? It is encased in magic dust. Those weeks were light and memorable, more so than the other months in that city. I wrote bits and pieces of my thesis on a rickety wooden table in our backyard and allowed myself to get sunburned at every opportunity. In winter we stayed layered up and indoors, but summer invited us outside; it invited us to smile at strangers, to leave our coats hanging on their hooks and receive what the sun had to offer us as it melted away any remnant of cold.

One strikingly warm day in August, Erik and I sat in a sunny spot by the river near town. Erik was one of my nonchurch friends. I played volleyball with him a few times on a rec league through *Oxford* Oxford. After I learned that half the team was made up of six-foot-four Scandinavians and I was never going to successfully get the ball over my side of the net during practice, I quit. But I remained friends with some of the people, including Erik, one of the Scandinavians. He turned out to be much less intimidating when he wasn't ferociously blocking me.

Erik was in Oxford pursuing a degree in economics. He split his time equally between studying and pining over his girlfriend, Kari, back home in Norway, who was as blond and almost as tall as he was. Erik had crazy blue eyes that jumped around with every new thought that came to mind, and he compulsively pushed his hair back with his hand every five minutes until it was a mess of strands pointing various directions. His neck craned forward in a mad-scientist kind of way. He was one of those brilliant, lively, strange yet endearing characters one rarely meets in real life. I think part of the reason I liked hanging out with Erik was sheer entertainment of the caricature that he was.

Erik's father was a successful businessman. Whatever he did—it was never clear to me—he made enough money to send Erik to boarding schools, fancy camps in the summer, and a fully funded gap year that Erik seems to remember little of. I got the sense that he was away from home a lot in his growing-up years. Other than that, I didn't know Erik well.

I had suggested we bring a baguette and cheese to the riverbank one day in late summer as a belated birthday celebration for both of us. We shared June birthdays. The river was crowded with punting boats—shallow wooden boats, a little larger than canoes—that were available to rent by the hour. The boats don't have paddles; instead, someone stands in the stern and guides the boat with a large pole that drags along the riverbed, similar to guiding a gondola. When several punters are out at once, the river becomes a stage for their choreography. The lifting and lowering of the poles. One boat gliding this way, the other that way. Entering and exiting stage right and then stage left. The sound of water moving slowly. It's hypnotizing. The boats crisscrossed on the water in front of us, and I told Erik about my recent trip home and the job offer in Nashville.

"Congratulations," he said. "Must be nice to know what you'll be doing when you get home."

"Yeah, it really is. Thanks."

Erik—the wild-eyed, crazy-haired Erik that I knew—seemed subdued.

"What about you?" I asked. "What are your plans for when you finish your degree?"

"I'll be moving home."

"You will? I didn't know that. Are you excited?"

"No," he laughed.

"Why not?"

"Home right now is . . . let's just say I'd rather stay here." He smiled sadly.

"Oh, I'm sorry."

"Stuff back home is complicated with my family. My father is retired now. I cannot imagine that man not working. I cannot imagine both of my parents at home with each other all day."

"Hmm."

"I've never had to face any of it. I've always been at school or traveling or somewhere else. Now, I don't have an excuse. I want to be where Kari is and Kari is, unfortunately, where my parents are."

"Yeah."

"I don't know what it is exactly. Every time I think of going home, I get tense. What is that? And my grandmother's living with them right now. That's an entirely different subject. I'll come home and show her my master of philosophy in economics from Oxford University and the first thing she'll say is, 'So when will you receive your doctorate?'"

I began to feel uncomfortable as Erik spoke. I shifted around in the grass. Nodded my head kindly. I tried to listen, but I didn't like it. The real talk, the openness. Erik and I had not done this before. Our friendship to this point had remained on the surface. It was light, fun, and sporadic. But as Erik revealed a more serious part of himself, caricature Erik began to look more like human Erik.

I wanted it to stop. I wanted Erik to remain a caricature because knowing he was real and getting a look into who he really was meant I would care about him more. And caring about him more meant I needed to have real conversations with him. And real conversations with him meant I needed to be my real self, my real, Jesus-loving, Christian self.

I don't want nonbelievers to go through difficult seasons or to have bad feelings or problems. I know that sounds strange, but I don't want them to have issues because I don't know how to help them with that. I don't know how they could ever cope outside the context of my own belief system. I don't know what sort of advice to give. I have no solutions for them aside from the hope that comes from the gospel. For this reason, I like to pretend they don't have feelings. It's easier for me this way. I don't feel as responsible or as needed in their lives if I pretend their thoughts and emotions never make it to the deep end. But here was Erik, exposing his real self to me and forcing me to empathize and to care. The nerve.

Typically, when friends are sharing something real with me, I dive in. I attack them with questions and try to help figure out a way they can work through things or at least how we can pray about it together. I say phrases like, "God will carry you through this. He has before, and he will again," "God is with you," "Trust him." But I was more reserved around my nonchurch friends in Oxford. Instead of jumping in, I made circles on the surface of the water with my big toe, thinking a lot but saying little. I listened, but I harnessed my evangelical responses. I stayed far away from the language of my church upbringing. I wasn't home. I was here, in Oxford, sitting with this person who was like a tiny island, off the coast of nowhere, near the edge of the universe.

Should I have been so careful? Would it have been so bad to be me in that moment? Would it have offended him to use words like "journey" and "hope" and "peace" and "season"? Did I have to tiptoe on eggshells as lightly as I did?

No, I don't think so now. But I did what I had been doing in conversations with friends like Erik for nearly a year. I expressed concern but said nothing about Jesus and real hope. In response to Erik's outpouring, I tore off a piece of baguette. I held it in my hand and simply said, "I'm sorry."

I cycled past the Martyrs' Memorial countless times that year, but I never stopped to really study it. It was built to memorialize three martyrs of the Protestant Reformation: Thomas Cranmer, former archbishop of Canterbury; Nicholas Ridley, former bishop of London; and Hugh Latimer, former bishop of Worcester. The memorial stands tall on the south end of St. Giles Street, just as city center is coming into view. A cross balances at the very top, capping off a steeple-like structure engraved with an ornate Gothic design that gives the whole thing an air of importance and seriousness. Statues of the three martyrs guard the memorial from pedestals on every side. Cranmer faces north and holds a Bible. Ridley faces south and stares stoically ahead. Latimer faces east. His back slightly hunched, giving the impression he may topple over at any moment.

All three men were burned at the stake for refusing to renounce their Protestant faith and pledge allegiance to the pope in the mid-

1500s under the reign of Mary Tudor, better known as Bloody Mary. The memorial, however, wasn't built until the nineteenth century, and it is quite something, standing seventy-three feet tall, surrounded by a thick base of stairs—a miniature, 360-degree Spanish Steps, if you will, where people lounge and eat their lunches beneath the shadows of the historic reformers.

You can't walk around Oxford proper without noticing the memorial, admiring it, stopping to read what it's about. It makes its presence known. It is sturdy and strong. It's been standing for over 170 years, and I'm sure it will be standing for a long time to come.

Cranmer's, Ridley's, and Latimer's stories are ones of bold words and brave acts. They went up against Bloody Mary, giving their lives to a cause. They held some controversial beliefs at the time: justification through faith instead of works, Scripture's authority over the pope, and the right to read the Bible in the common tongue. In Oxford everybody knows this is what these men stood for, and their brave deaths are forever commemorated.

I, like Ridley, Latimer, and Cranmer, am also a Protestant. And that is the one and only thing we have in common.

I did not speak boldly in Oxford. I had little resolve. I put an immense amount of pressure on the way I behaved in conversations with my friends who had different beliefs, and I consistently felt like a failure. Let's just come right out and say it: I did not once share the gospel with a nonbeliever while in Oxford. I thought about it. I planned out conversations in my head. I wondered which verses I should use or what arguments I could make that would stand up to theirs. But when it came down to it, I just never did. And for that, I felt like an incredibly lousy evangelist.

I felt undeserving to stand under the great fathers of the faith that year, so I cycled by the Martyrs' Memorial without a glance. If I had ever stopped, I would have parked myself right beneath the men's statues and whispered an apology.

"I'm sorry," I'd say. "I've failed you. I've failed our faith."

Silence from the men above.

"You professed your beliefs so boldly. Look at you guys. An entire monument was built in your honor. I can't even speak half the time. I'm about as far from a martyr as they come."

Silence.

"I mean, Cranmer, you must be so ashamed of me. You wrote the Book of Common Prayer *and* you were burned at the stake. You're a saint. Wait, you might actually be a saint. Are you a saint?"

Silence.

"No. Of course you're not. The whole Protestant thing. I forgot. See, I don't even know the doctrines of my own religion anymore . . .

"Cranmer, oh great father of the faith, why have I been so quiet this year? Do you think there's something wrong with me?"

Erik and I got up from our spot by the river and made our way to our bikes chained up in an alley a block away. As we walked, I felt overcome by guilt and regret. I regretted being so quiet and not saying anything about Jesus or faith. I regretted this not only with him but with everyone else I crossed paths with in Oxford whom I'd failed to evangelize. Conversations, missed opportunities, silent moments I should have filled. Scripture left unmentioned. I regretted that I had let my Christian life take place only around certain people, and I began to panic because it was August. I was leaving in September. I was running out of time in Oxford. I needed to do something, and I needed to do it fast.

I had missed my chances with others, but maybe Erik would be my saving grace, as long as he was saved. Maybe this was my redeeming moment that would undo any shame or passivity or fear I had felt in the previous months. All of it would be justified with this life-changing conversation Erik and I were about to have on a street in Oxford.

Feeling heavy with the weight of the gospel, I stopped walking.

"Hey!" I said.

Erik, startled, stopped and looked at me. "What?"

"There's something you should know about me."

"Okay . . ."

"I'm a Christian."

"I know."

"Oh, you do?"

"Yeah, you always talk about going to do stuff at that church you go to in town."

"St. Aldates? Oh yeah. I do stuff there a lot. Well, I guess what I'm really wanting to say is, I'm sorry you have to go home to such a messy situation, and . . ."

"And?"

"I'm going to be praying for you."

He smiled. "Thank you, Andrea. I'm sure you mean that." He turned down the alley and walked toward his bike. I followed.

"I do. I mean it. I really believe in God and prayer and all of that and that it can help you. I really do."

"I believe you," he said, facing me again. "And I really do appreciate your saying that. I guess I'll be praying in my own way too."

"You will?"

"Yeah, you know. I'll keep my hopes up. I'll think positive thoughts. All that stuff. I'm not against your beliefs or anything. You know that, right?"

"Yeah, of course. You're very open minded. It's just—"

"I went to a monastery once when I was traveling through Spain."

"You did? How was it?"

"Peaceful. I like you Christian types." Oh yeah, peaceful. That's what we're supposed to be like.

I stood there not sure what to say, or not say, next. I looked at him intently. His face said he genuinely respected my beliefs, but he also genuinely did not desire to believe in it for himself. He was content. Really, genuinely content. In a way, more content than I was.

I had this understanding at the time, something I picked up from somewhere at some point, that my Christian faith made me different and that others would notice the difference and wonder what caused it. Then they would be drawn in by that difference and want what I had that they seemed to lack.

I think I secretly hoped the people I met in Oxford felt this way about me, as if my aura were irresistible. We'd go to coffee and they would look at me and say, "Andrea, there is something so different about you. Tell me what it is." And the door would be opened for me to share the gospel, and we would cry and read Scripture, and then someday I would write a book about all the people I helped bring to Christ in Oxford.

This is not what happened to me. In fact, as I noticed with Erik, I think I had the opposite effect on people.

"This is concerning." (I'm talking to Cranmer's statue again.) "I should be the content one, right? I'm the one who has the peace of God in me. I'm the one who lives by faith through grace, and yet, here I am with these people who are completely capable of feeling joy, sadness, and worry like I am, and those emotions don't make them wonder where they came from. Tough seasons don't make them want to turn to something greater for help. They don't feel the need. They don't have the desperation. It's like they've just accepted that life is life. If God is real, that's good. If he isn't, that's fine too. And you know what the real kicker is?"

Silence.

"I'm jealous. I'm jealous of their disinterest toward God."

It's true. I was. With Erik, and with a few others I knew during that time, I realized that instead of growing more fervent for others to see and believe and understand, I grew more understanding of why they didn't see or believe or understand. I began to want what they had.

If I could accept the lack of answers to my ever-growing list of questions about Scripture and the story of Jesus and who he is and was, if I could feel content with not being sure whether or not there was a purpose to this whole thing, a designer, an Adam and an Eve, a tree in a garden, a story about a Savior that's been told and retold until it trickled down to me. Oh, if only I could feel content. How the complications would fade, how the restless nights would soothe themselves into complacency.

"I know this sounds terrible, Cranmer, but I don't want to introduce people to the confusion of Christianity. I want their complacency. I see why they don't want to see."

Silence.

Right around the corner from where Cranmer and I are "talking" is Broad Street. And on Broad Street is another memorial. It's embedded right in the middle of the pavement—an unassuming collection of white- and slate-colored bricks that form the shape of a cross. They're laid neatly, even with the street. This cross marks the actual spot where Cranmer, Ridley, and Latimer were burned at the stake.

It is the opposite of the St. Giles Street memorial in every way. A small, plain, low-to-the-ground, blink-and-you-miss-it little sight. Typically, people walk right over it or right past it, but occasionally, a tourist pauses beside it—reading his guidebook—nods and moves on. It doesn't take long to inspect. It's a cluster of bricks.

No one is going to hang out Spanish Steps–style around the memorial on Broad Street. No one calls his friends and says, "Meet you at the Martyrs' Memorial, the one on Broad Street." That would be like saying, "Meet you by those weeds growing on the side of the road." No one would really know what you were talking about. Where? Which weeds? Is there something special or noteworthy about these certain weeds I've been overlooking all this time? And then you would just call your friend back and say, "Can we meet at the Martyrs' Memorial, the one on *St. Giles Street* instead?"

When I was studying abroad in undergrad, we visited both memorials during one of my Oxford Through the Ages lectures. (The same class that taught me about the haunting ghost of Saint Frideswide.) It's interesting. Despite the obvious physical disparity between the two memorials—one a seventy-three-foot, beautifully crafted structure, and the other bricks—I only recall visiting the Broad Street memorial. I asked some friends who took that class with me which memorial they remember. All of them remembered St. Giles Street, and none of them remembered Broad Street. I suppose for the exact reason it is so often overlooked, it stuck out to me that semester as one of the more remarkable Oxford sights. Such a tiny, seemingly insignificant spot that marks such a tragic and historical moment for Protestantism and the church.

When our professor gathered us around it on Broad Street, I felt like I had been let in on a secret of some kind. Here we were standing in the middle of a busy road staring at the ground as people passed us by. We were looking at basically nothing, but we were discussing martyrdom, dying for the cause of Christ. Something like that, when you think about it, can never be paid tribute in full. No statue, no matter how grand, could be enough. The memorial where Cranmer stands on St. Giles Street was a grand gesture, but the memorial on Broad Street, in my opinion, is a truer one.

Back in the alley, Erik got on his bike and looked back at me. He was ready to leave, and I was ready to let him.

"See you, Andrea. Thanks for the prayer."

"See you, Erik. Anytime."

I hopped on my bike and rode down all the familiar streets. The road looked the same as it always did. It was not colored in the light of saving souls, but it was colored in the light of having been a truer version of myself. And who's to say being yourself isn't its own type of evangelism anyway?

In his book *The Pilgrimage,* Paulo Coelho details his experience on the renowned Camino de Santiago, a five-hundred-mile walk through France and Spain that takes about thirty days to complete. At one point his mentor, Petrus, tells him, "We are always trying to convert people to a belief in our own explanation of the universe. We think that the more people there are who believe as we do, the more certain it will be that what we believe is the truth. But it doesn't work that way at all."[9]

Maybe all this time, in his silence, Cranmer had been trying to point me away from himself and toward something else. I had been wasting my time here with him. I needed to round the corner to Broad Street, kneel down, and consider the bricks. When I get there, I crouch down and touch one of the bricks. It is cool and smooth. Many feet have been here.

The trek from the St. Giles Street memorial to the Broad Street memorial is 0.1 mile. I don't know that a tenth of a mile is worthy of the title "pilgrimage," but what if it takes one year to travel that 0.1 mile? Surely that is a worthy pilgrimage. When the way there is crooked and winding, it requires more time. More nights of wine and darkness and hope and laughter, the entire time being led, quietly, by someone bigger, stronger, and more all knowing than you on a pilgrimage you've unknowingly set out upon.

The crooked way is not the bad way. In fact, I think the crooked way is the only way. Detours, nooks, turns, and dead ends house the places where we learn, grow, and are strengthened, where our weak beliefs turn into something stronger, sturdier, and less wavering. In the crookedness is our true tale and our real selves—things we would never find on the straight and narrow.

Simple bricks, tall statues. Aren't we all made up of the same stuff

9. Paulo Coelho, *The Pilgrimage: A Contemporary Quest for Ancient Wisdom* (HarperSan-Francisco, 1995), 92.

in the end? Materials laid carefully, differently but purposefully. Sometimes we are quiet for entire seasons, entire years. And sometimes we are loud and bold and want others to see his glory. Maybe no statues have been raised in your honor in the towns that you've left, but why can't footprints be enough? A tennis shoe imprinted in the mud. Fingertips brushed along an old cement wall. Dirty dishes in the sink. Worn-down bicycle tires. Your scent left floating in the air as you walk from room to room. An "Andrea was here" scratched in the bathroom stall. A movie stub that fell from your pocket and others stepped on. Words said and unsaid. Perhaps we can leave our marks without actually leaving a mark.

I smiled as I left Erik that day, not because I had been a successful evangelist, but because I realized that such an honest and raw me did not exist a year earlier. I cared too much about what everybody thought, and I doubted too much what I was saying. As I pedaled home the ice dripped off my shoulders and splashed to the ground beneath me, revealing what had been lying in wait, frozen. And I liked what I saw.

I rode down all the familiar streets with the romantic-sounding names. Magdalen Road turned onto Iffley Road. Iffley Road turned onto Donnington Bridge. And Donnington Bridge curved into home. Like it always does. I hopped off my bike, pulled it around the back of the house, and locked it up. I went in the back door and made myself a cup of tea. The kettle rattled with the boil, and I tipped it over into my small mug to turn the water a murky brown.

I don't know where all the people are now whom I met and knew so briefly in Oxford. Life has rippled on for me as it has for them, but I hope we remember the brief moment in which our waters took an unexpected turn, met each other, and then parted again.

12

Pillars

In many ways Oxford is the not real place. Time feels suspended there. Everything around you looks dreamy. The old buildings, the churches, the colleges. Surely none of it is real. Surely nothing that old is still that beautiful. Surely the grass is not that green all year round. Surely the quaintest of trails in the most obscure of parks does not sweep you up into another time, another era. But it did, and it does. Oxford, the not real place.

·⌒·

I met Biceps, as I will call him, close to when I was due to move back to the States. It was well after Jisu, after the river conversation, and after another conversation Jisu and I had at an ice-cream shop—a setting much too cheerful for the discussion at hand. It was after I had given up hope of bringing home a British husband or having a chance encounter with Prince Harry.

I met Biceps at an interesting time, and just in time, but also when I was running out of time. Time, though, for whatever reason, suspended itself for us, me and Biceps. After I met him and in the weeks following, days seemed to slow down, stretch out, elongate. Time lifted us out of its rushing waters for a little while. In summer, the British sun takes its sweet time before setting each day. We told ourselves to not worry about the future. The future was not allowed to bother us, not just yet. We were protected inside Oxford's walls, inside time suspended.

Biceps wasn't British. He was American and a coworker of Lizzy's. He had been a member of Oxford's power-lifting team and it showed, in a good way, hence his nickname. I noticed his biceps right after I noticed his eyes, which was right after I noticed his smile. I met him at Lizzy's birthday party where we had a nice little candid conversation about faith.

We were at a bar where you sit on cushions on the floor and lamps hang occasionally from the ceiling. The room was dark and covered with Persian rugs. I chose a cushion beside Biceps because, you know, biceps.

"So how did you end up living with Lizzy?" he asked.

"I saw her ad for a roommate on my church's website."

"Oh, so you go to church. You're a Christian like Lizzy?"

Annnd here we go, I thought. "Yeah, I am."

"Cool. I grew up going to church."

"You did?"

"Yeah. Baptist. Southern Baptist."

"Oh. I haven't met many Southern Baptists over here. Where do you go to church in Oxford?"

"Not really anywhere. I haven't gone to church in a while."

"Oh. Sorry, I just assumed you might. I shouldn't assume everyone who grew up in church still goes to church."

"It's okay. My theology has changed quite a bit since I've lived here actually."

"How so?"

"I came here five years ago to study just that, theology. I went to Regent's Park"—I knew Regent's Park. It was *Oxford* Oxford and known for its courses in theology and philosophy—"and as I got into it . . . I don't know. The more I studied it, the less it made sense, so I started experimenting."

"Experimenting? With what?"

"Theology."

"Oh."

"I was an atheist for a little while, then an agnostic for a long time. But now, now, I'm more of a liberal Christian."

"A liberal Christian? What does that mean?"

For some reason this made him laugh.

"I guess it means I like Jesus. I like what he taught. He was a good teacher, and I want to be a good person, like he was."

"Hmm."

I wasn't sure what to think of this "liberal Christianity" he spoke of. It sounded like a way to follow Jesus without believing in him, and I wasn't sure what the point of that was, but I was intrigued.

Biceps and I kept seeing each other after that night. When I think about our time together, some of our moments were so stupidly perfect they could have been in a movie. Our own movie, set in Oxford, the not real place.

```
FADE IN:
INT. A BURRITO RESTAURANT—NIGHT
Biceps and Andrea have empty plates in front
of them. They are sitting across from each
other at a table.
```

BICEPS

```
So where is this big publishing job you're off
to when you get back home?
```

ANDREA

```
It's not a BIG publishing job. I'm just going to
be an editorial assistant.
```

BICEPS

I'm sure it will become a big job.

ANDREA

(Laughs) I hope so. It's in Nashville. I've only been there a couple of times and once was for the interview. I don't know anybody there. Is it kind of crazy to move somewhere for a job you don't know how to do in a place where you don't know anybody?

BICEPS

Nah, that's how life works half the time. You didn't really know anybody in Oxford when you moved here, right?

ANDREA

Yeah, that's true. Have you ever been to Nashville?

BICEPS

Yeah, I've been there a lot actually. My hometown is just an hour and a half away.

ANDREA

No way. It is?

BICEPS

Yeah, we used to go to the big city all the time on the weekends. It's a fun place. You'll like it.

ANDREA

I hope so. What is your hometown like?

BICEPS

My hometown? It's hardly a town. It's farmland. Everywhere you look, land, cattle, corn.

ANDREA

That sounds nice.

BICEPS

I guess so. If you like that sort of thing. Biceps picks up his glass and pauses before taking a sip.

BICEPS

I might be moving back actually. Andrea, who is about to take a sip of her water, freezes, her cup midair.

ANDREA

Really? You might be moving back to the town

that's an hour and a half from the town I'm moving to?

BICEPS

I know. What are the odds, right? I might have an opportunity there. I thought I would stay in England a while longer, but now, I don't know. Life might be taking me back home.

They sit at the table for a long time, talking. When people begin sweeping the floors around them, they reluctantly stand up to leave.

BICEPS

Do you want to ride our bikes home or walk?

ANDREA

Let's walk.

EXT. THE BURRITO RESTAURANT

It's nearly midnight now. The streets are wet. It had rained while Biceps and Andrea were inside. At midnight under streetlamps and where everything is shiny with damp, the city looks ridiculously romantic.

CAMERA ZOOMS OUT TO AERIAL VIEW

Andrea and Biceps pass St. Mary's Church and walk their bikes along Magdalen Bridge. They wonder how they had possibly come to meet each other, here, in Oxford. Where they had both traveled so far to come.

They stop at the street where Biceps lives. They stand with their bikes between them.

BICEPS

This was fun. We'll have to close down the burrito place again sometime.

ANDREA

Yeah, I would like that.

BICEPS

Good night, Andrea.

ANDREA

Good night, Biceps.

Biceps pushes his bike and hops on the seat while it's still moving—a seamless, athletic move that impresses Andrea. She watches him ride away.

FADE OUT

It was all adding up. We were both moving to the South. We had found each other in Oxford, of all places. The timing of it was like a fairy tale. But the audience knows that when things are going really well, they are going too well. Meeting Biceps felt like a wonderful and miraculous stroke of fate, with a hint of impending disaster. I knew that although we were in the same place physically, we weren't really in the same place . . . spiritually. The whole Jesus thing. The whole liberal thing, and the fact I still wasn't sure what that meant. These were things I knew I needed to consider, and I would, but not yet. Not in Oxford, our not real place.

One night, Biceps made me dinner at his house. After we ate, we sat on his couch and began our second bottle of wine for the evening.

"Let me try to understand this," I said. "You came to Oxford to get your master's in religious studies, and then you started questioning exactly what you were studying?"

"That's the gist, yeah."

"But, I don't get it. I mean, you were in all the apologetics classes. You studied the Word, and your professors convinced you to not believe?"

"I didn't really take apologetics classes. I did take classes about the origin of the Bible though. People, men, regular old men, decided what went into that book. They had agendas, just like people in politics have agendas when they pass or don't pass a law. It was all just pieced together. The whole thing. The whole book our Sunday school teachers told us we should base our entire lives on."

I took two sips of wine and pulled one leg under the other, facing him.

"That would mess me up. To learn all that stuff. I guess I would rather not know?"

"Really? But how can you follow something if you don't understand it or know where it all comes from? You don't seem like the type of girl who wants to be spoon-fed religion."

"I don't. I . . . I'm not. But . . . wait, I have more questions for you."

Biceps laughed. He was really enjoying this.

"You claim to follow Jesus, but you don't believe what Scripture says about him, that he was the Son of God—"

"Wait, wait, wait. I didn't say that exactly. I'm not sure about what Scripture says about him. I'm not sure he was the Son of God, and I'm not sure we can be sure, based on what we have in front of us. And I think I've finally come to a place in my life where I'm okay with not being sure. I'm okay with not knowing."

"'Okay with not being sure,'" I repeated slowly. "I'm not sure I'm okay with that."

"Yeah." Biceps smiled. "I can see that."

I sighed. "Let's talk about something else."

"No, I love talking about this stuff. I want to know what you think."

Biceps put his wine glass down and looked directly at me. He had blue eyes and blond hair and the straightest, whitest teeth I had ever seen. In my opinion, he could have been a model, and the intensity of his attention, his eyes on me, his body pointed toward mine, sometimes made me forget what he said. Sometimes it made the words coming out of his mouth evaporate into inaudible sounds, like someone had just put my life on mute.

I thought he was too good looking for me. I thought he needed someone prettier or more petite or more blond than I was, someone who was not wearing the same old Converse tennis shoes she wore every other day. But here we were, together, sitting on his couch, and I was the one he was looking at.

After a second I came to.

"What I think about what?" I asked.

"Everything. Scripture, Jesus. What has it been like to be a Christian from Texas in a place like Oxford?"

"Well, it's been good and hard and weird and a lot of things."

"Great, tell me about it."

"Okay . . . It's been hard spiritually because I've doubted, like seriously, for the first time, doubted what I believe about God and Christianity and stuff."

"Yeah? Keep going."

I took another sip of wine.

"So, when I got here, I realized so much of what I believe I only believed because it was what I was taught. Being here, in this other country where so many smart people are just sort of running around everywhere, I realized they weren't raised like I was. And I wondered if I would have turned out like them if I hadn't been raised in Texas, by Christian parents, in a Christian home."

"Yes. Exactly. I know how you feel. Okay, keep going."

"Keep going?"

"Yeah. Just talk."

No one had ever told me to do that before. Just talk. I had done a lot of listening in my life. A lot of sitting back, watching, observing. Going away and journaling my thoughts on pages no one would ever see or read. I hadn't done much of my own talking. Maybe because I didn't feel like it was safe to. I had thoughts, lots of thoughts, but I couldn't say them out loud to just anybody. Biceps was beginning to feel safe for out-loud talking. He didn't seem to fear what I had to say. Sometimes, when I talked out loud with good church people about my doubts or when I asked them questions about the Bible, I felt them hold my words at bay. They didn't let them in and think about them and mull them over. Some of them even seemed afraid.

I remember having a conversation with a guy I had recently met. He was a Christian and really smart, so I assumed it was safe for me to bring up some questions I had about certain passages in Scripture. I had been wrestling with what the Bible said about a certain topic. Christians seemed split on the issue too, so I did a little research. I read arguments from both sides, and I prayed about it. As I was explaining my processing and my wrestling to this guy, he interrupted me.

"Wait," he said. "Don't tell me you even considered believing those passages in Scripture weren't true or relevant."

"Uh, well, yeah I guess I did, sorta—"

"Wow, Andrea. I mean, I'm a sinner. I know what it's like to be in the depth and pit of sin, but if I ever got to the point where I was questioning the very Word of God, well, that would be a dark place to be. I would doubt what sort of God I professed to believe in, in the first place. I would doubt if I believed in the Christian God at all."

I was stunned. I didn't know what to say. I walked away from that conversation not only still doubting that particular passage of Scripture but also doubting myself and my legitimacy as a Christian.

Biceps could not have been more the opposite of this guy and the others who fear the doubter. He did not hold my words at bay. He did not suggest I needed prayer. He did not suggest that I was in the darkest place a Christian could ever be and I should probably be questioning everything at this point. Instead, he listened to me. He looked at me. He said without actually saying it that I could say all the things that were in my head, and he would not feel afraid. With him, and with very few others I've come across in life, I felt safe in the sphere of "just talk."

So I told him all about the friends I'd met in my classes at Brookes. I told him how their depth had surprised me. How their capacity to love was so strong. I told him how I had seen how they loved their significant others and their friends and their families, with a fierce type of love, a trustworthy type. And I told him that I wondered if atheists and agnostics were better at loving people than Christians were because love here on earth was all they had. The people around them were it, their entire world. Maybe they felt an urgency to love that those who believe in and are counting on the afterlife do not.

Biceps sat there and listened to me and nodded. I couldn't believe I was telling him all this, but I kept going. I wanted to keep going.

"So these people weren't raised as Christians, but I was. And I was thinking about that, and how I don't think I would be a Christian if I had been raised in England. There's no way. There's just no way. I mean, look at me. Two weeks into this place and I was saying, 'I don't even know if I believe in God anymore.' But . . ."

"But?"

"Well, I had this thought the other day."

"What thought?"

"Maybe God knew that about me."

"Knew what?"

"That I shouldn't grow up in England. That I needed my parents and their faith and the faith of those around me because it would have been too hard for me here."

Biceps nodded his head but didn't say anything.

"Maybe I wasn't ready for England until now, now that I'm older."

He laughed.

"Okay, maybe I'm not twenty-seven like you, but I'm not seventeen anymore."

"No, I know. I know what you mean. Continue."

"I was going to."

Biceps tilted his head, surprised by my snark. He swept one hand out with a "by all means" gesture. I cleared my throat.

"If God created me, he created me with a questioning and curious mind. He knew a place like Oxford would be hard for me. I couldn't have believed in my faith without the support of my family and friends and people around me. But now, well, Jesus is in me. I don't think there's anything I can do about that. I think he's just there. And I wasn't sure at first when I got here, but I've heard him. I've seen him work. I've seen him at my church and in my own heart. In big and little things. I get why you're not a Christian anymore—"

"Hey—"

"Okay, sorry. Why you're not a 'conservative' Christian anymore, or whatever. But that's not me. At least, I don't think it is. And maybe it is just comforting to believe, and maybe I need to study more, but . . . I don't know. Maybe I don't."

"Hmm, yeah. Maybe you don't. Maybe I shouldn't have. But it's too late now."

We sat quietly for a while. I wondered if it was too late. I wondered if I was being naive in my faith. I wondered how much power we have over our own beliefs and over our own disbeliefs in the end. I wondered how deep biblical study can create people like John Lennox and people like Biceps at the same time.

"I still love God," Biceps said finally. "I know that sounds strange, but I do. I talk to him. I've been talking to him more these days."

"I know you love him. I can tell you do. And I'm glad you still talk to him."

"Yeah."

"Yeah."

"Well, it's getting late," Biceps said.

"Oh, you're right, it is. I'm sorry."

"What are you sorry for?"

"I . . . I don't know. Talking too much?"

Biceps smiled.

"You didn't talk too much. Come on, I'll walk you home."

```
FADE IN:
NIGHT. IN FRONT OF ANDREA'S HOUSE ON DONNINGTON
BRIDGE
The night is cold and you can see Andrea's and
Biceps's breath as they say good night. He
kisses her on the cheek. Andrea doesn't move.
Biceps jumps on his bike and is off before she
can say anything.
```

Port Meadow was glowing. Port Meadow is always glowing, but especially that day, the day Biceps and I rode our bikes through it under the sun, when we knew it would rain soon but not just yet. The ground was preparing to receive it, and the blades of grass seemed to be growing, craning their necks back and opening their tiny mouths.

Port Meadow is an actual meadow, like the ones they write about in children's stories with bunnies. The meadow, by law, can never be developed, and this has been the law since the land was gifted to Oxford by Alfred the Great in the tenth century.

The meadow is big, so so big, and very flat with mounds of grass and bumpy, muddy trails over here and over there. Oversized blackberry bushes line the east side of it, and as you trek farther west, depending on how far you are willing to walk, you might run into the smallest and most charming abandoned church you've ever seen. The Thames is nearby at all times, but at some point it disappears and then reappears when you get close to a pub called The Trout Inn, our destination that afternoon.

The Trout was busy. Most tables inside were taken, so we found two cushiony chairs in an interior room near the fireplace. We could hear the rain on the roof, the rain we had known was coming. It was hard, but it wouldn't last long. Hard rain like that in England comes and goes before you have time to complain about it or bother to pull out an umbrella.

The Trout has been around since the seventeenth century, and it is the type of pub you imagine novels have been written in and where very important, slightly drunken conversations have probably taken place over the last several hundred years.

Like the night after dinner on his couch and like the very first night we met, my conversation with Biceps turned to faith quickly. This, I was learning, was his favorite topic.

Biceps sat on the edge of his seat with his elbows on his knees.

"So, Andrea, what are your pillars?"

"My pillars?"

"You know, what you believe. What holds up your faith. Your pillars."

"Oh, my pillars . . ." I drew back in my chair and crossed my arms.

In my mind little scenes from the past year flickered on and off:

- riding my bike home late at night and feeling what it would be like to be God-less
- feeling that for the first time
- fasting during Lent and hating every second of it
- attempting to leave Oxford early, before I would have ever met Biceps
- Ben walking away from me at the library
- my little "conversation" with Thomas Cranmer
- sitting here with a "liberal" Christian while Jisu was who knows where

Could I really state my pillars now? In such a state? Was I the right person to be doing this? I wanted to invite someone else down to say them for me. Maybe I could get my dad on the phone and ask him, and he could say it. I could just stand there, and when he was done, I would point my thumb and say, "Yeah, what he said." But Biceps didn't want to know what my friends' or family's pillars were. He wanted to know mine. So, clumsily and with no eloquence at all, I began to recite my creed.

"Jesus is the Son of God . . ."

"Yeah, okay."

"And he came here to die for us."

"Mmhm."

"Because of him, what he did on the cross, because of that, I will spend eternity with God. I don't deserve to, but I will."

Under Biceps's watchful eye, I felt uncertain.

"You sure about all that?"

"Yeah, yeah I think I am. I have to be."

"You don't have to be."

I didn't want him to be right about that, but he was. I didn't have to be sure, not right then.

I read something singer-songwriter Derek Webb wrote recently. He was confessing and apologizing for some mistakes he had made the previous year. I am sure there was nothing easy about writing it. I loved something he wrote at the end:

> I've said recently that my songs feel like my personal liturgy, things that I don't necessarily or always believe but I show up to recite again and again in hopes of believing them. If I'm honest, most of the time I don't believe the words in my songs. I have a hard time believing in a God that could make, let alone love a man who could do such things. So, I'll go on reciting and adding to my liturgy in hopes of believing the words, because I wish to. More than ever, I wish to.[10]

Maybe, sitting on a leather chair that afternoon in The Trout, I was not 100 percent all in and all certain about my "pillars," but saying them aloud is something I've never forgotten. I was shaky and not confident. I was unnerved by the smart Oxford graduate across from

10. Derek Webb, "On Failure, Liturgy, and New Years," Facebook, January 1, 2016, www .facebook.com/derekwebb/posts/10156423125900512 (also republished on *Relevant*, January 4, 2016, www.relevantmagazine.com/life/ derek-webb-failure-liturgy-and-new-years).

me, but I said it, and sometimes saying it out loud is all we can do. Sometimes reciting the Creed we are uncertain about is what leads us to eventual certainty, or at least to a deeper assurance. This is why we write and sing hymns. This is why we read one book over and over and over again. Words—remembering them, saying them, and writing them—are foundational for us. Our words make up who we are. They are not only powerful; they are, I think, our only power.

Biceps had studied Scripture more than I had. He had received his master's in theology, and that was where he had begun to doubt the absolute of Scripture on a serious and deep level. Right in the middle of breathing it in, he saw the holes, the humanness of it. Things were left out. Groups of people—sinful, normal people—had decided what would go in. Jesus was a wonderful teacher, and the Bible a wonderful book, but is it alive? Is it more than moral teaching? Was Jesus more than a rabbi? These were questions Biceps no longer answered with an affirmative yes. He was a man who loved God a lot, I could tell. I didn't doubt that. But his mind was fighting with his heart and with his past and the things he had been told to believe in. They didn't fit in this country of England. So few beliefs, when they traverse an ocean, make the trip without minor damage.

I had, with great uncertainty, remembered my words. In the foreign land, I had remembered them. Across from this person, I was saying them, and though the doubt had been painful at times, the faith underneath was indeed proving more durable. Maybe I recited my words to Biceps that day, but I recited them for me.

Outside The Trout I could hear the river. It was slowing down as the rain let up. And I thought about how the river had witnessed many important events for me that year, and the thought comforted me greatly.

On our walk home, we talked about lighter things. Biceps asked me why I was still single and who I had dated in Oxford. No one, was the correct and truest answer, but I found myself telling him about Jisu. All about my good friend Jisu. I told him he was the closest I had come to dating anyone that year but in the end it just didn't work out.

"Why not?" he asked. And just then on our Oxford movie set, it began to rain again.

```
FADE IN:
EXT. PORT MEADOW-DAY
Biceps and Andrea run their bikes under the
nearest tree to protect themselves from the
rain that is falling harder and harder.

                    BICEPS
Wow, it's really coming down now!

                    ANDREA
I know. Ugh, Oxford. It'll be over in a few
minutes.

                    BICEPS
Yeah.
They wait under the tree for a while. The tree
```

is large, and its branches curve all the way to the ground on one side. Nature's perfect umbrella. The sky is bright in some spots and dark in others. Unpredictable.

Andrea looks expectantly at Biceps. Biceps smiles but looks away. They stand still and quiet and watch.

The rain lightens.

BICEPS

Oh, good. I think it's clear enough to head back now.

Biceps mounts his bike and starts down a trail beside the river.

ANDREA

(whispers) Oh, good.

13

Good-Byes at Kazbar

A friend of my sister's once told her you must grieve everything. Any time you have to say good-bye to something, someone, or some place, grieve it. But how does one grieve? How does one set out, voluntarily, on an honest path of loss? The absolute last path anyone ever wants to set out upon. I'm not sure about the entire journey, but I am certain of the first step. Say the good-bye. Actually say the word, and then the words that need to be said before it and after it. Articulate it. Make it real, for yourself and, if the good-bye is to someone else, for the other person too. If words need to be said, say them. If they need to be written, write them. Whatever you need to do. Imagine that person in five years, and think about what you want him to remember about you and your relationship, and set a time and place for you to tell that person those things.

If you don't, if you don't say a real good-bye, you'll live in denial, refusing to acknowledge that this part of your life or this person in your life is no longer there. This denial suspends her—the person, place, or thing—in your mind. The person is gone, but she's not gone, for how can someone really be gone if you've never admitted she is? And thus you create an unnecessary ghost.

I wish I had said good-bye, really said good-bye, to all the important people in my life who are no longer a part of it for one reason or another. I have said it a handful of times, and I'm so glad I did. Like with my grandmother, not too long ago. I sat by her bed, knowing it would probably be the last time I saw her. She couldn't talk back, but I told her I loved her. I told her she had been a good grandmother, and then I told her that she made really good pies. I'm not sure why I went there, why I started talking about pie, but I did. I told her that her classic southern "all-good" pie was the best there was and I had always loved it. I felt a little foolish talking to her about pie in the last minutes that we were together, but in the moment pie was what I felt I needed to discuss and thank her for. It was a simple way of telling my grandmother that she had taken care of us well, that she had cooked for us so many times in a way that only a loving grandmother can, and that I would always remember her for her love and for her care. I wasn't able to say all of that sitting beside her bed that day. For some reason, that felt too hard. But I'm glad I at least talked to her about her pie. I think if she was able to hear what I was saying, she understood. I think she got it.

I haven't always taken the time to do the proper good-bye though. To sit down with someone and look at him. I wish I had. I wish I had said good-bye to Jisu. Really said good-bye.

I'm better at saying good-bye to things than to actual people. I'm sure we all are. Maybe this is why I orchestrated an Epic Good-Bye Walk around Oxford before I moved to Nashville. I planned it all out. A list of places I wanted to visit or look at one last time. It would be a long walk. It would take all day, and I would go alone. Going on good-bye walks alone is a completely normal thing to do.

The walk began at my little white house on Donnington Bridge. It was fall again. September. The month I had arrived one year before. My route was long and crooked, not efficient in any way, taking me to the pretty, hidden, and memorable parts of the city. The first part of my walk took me up Headington Hill on Divinity Road to the Brookes campus. A couple of days earlier, I had ridden my bike up the same street to submit my thesis.

Finishing my thesis was a feat I was only 10 percent sure I would be able to complete when I began graduate school. I remember during my first Shakespeare class, the professor warned us, "If you have not completed the required reading for this class at least twice by now, you are already behind."

I stared at the list in front of me. Ten plays. I had read three of them in undergrad, maybe, and only once. I called my mom after class and asked if I could fly home. Fortunately, she knew one class, and my tendency to overreact, was not reason enough to abandon graduate school altogether. She talked me into staying for at least another week or two.

I don't know if I had ever been as proud of myself as when I handed in that fifty-page paper on "The Role of Sacrifice in Postcolonial Literature." I printed it, dropped it in the appropriate box, and walked back to my bike weighing four hundred pounds less than when I arrived on campus that morning. It was finished. My master's done, forever. I never had to take another class or test or fake my way through a presentation on a literary topic I didn't actually understand. I would never, ever have to cite another source in the proper format. The thesis, the looming, how-will-I-ever-finish-it thesis, had been written.

I rode my bike down Headington Hill and can still remember exactly how the wind felt. Cold was returning to Oxford, though it had never really left. I could feel it on my scalp as the breeze cut through. My knuckles stiffened against the wind, but my face, usually held down to avoid full exposure, was lifted up this time. I was so thankful for all of it. The cold wind, the breeze, the hill. I rode it fast, and for a moment I saw me on the side of the road walking up the hill exactly one year before, headed to orientation.

Because this "past" me had left too early and given herself too much time to get there, she walked slowly, not wanting to be the first to arrive. Her slow pace gave her more time to take it in, to learn her route, the landmarks, to stare at the people walking past her, more sure of their footing than she was. She had left her parents waving at the bottom of the hill. The climb was steep, and she was worried she would be sweaty by the time she arrived to meet her teachers and her classmates. She was twenty-two years old, but felt eleven.

This September day, the day she would turn in her thesis, was far from her thoughts a year earlier. She didn't think it would actually come. As far as she was concerned in that moment, she would never survive this foreign country or all the papers she had to write. She didn't know she would get a job at the end of this all the way in Nashville or that she would make friends with unlikely people who taught her things she didn't know she needed to learn.

I rode down the hill faster and faster, and the image of me walking up faded. It was a small thing—to achieve a master's degree in England—but it was the absolute biggest thing then.

On my Epic Good-Bye Walk, I carried a camera and took pictures of the leaves in the trees on Divinity Road. It felt nice to walk without purpose, not rushing to get to class or get to the library before it closed. I watched students with their bags pass by me quickly on foot and on their bicycles. Once I got to the top of the hill, I looked at the building where my English classes were held. I looked at it for a minute, took a breath, and then took a sharp left toward South Park. The ever-grassy, beautiful South Park with the best view of the city below. I took a picture of the distant buildings and a moss-covered bench nearby and kept walking at my leisurely pace along Mesopotamia Walk, a footpath that takes you over the River Cherwell and through what looks and feels like a forest until, suddenly, you are in University Parks. The park where I jumped in the river years before.

From there it was more paths, crooked, then straight, crooked, then straight. A street, small at first, that opened onto Banbury Road, the road that led me into the city center of Oxford. I walked on Cornmarket Street in the middle of a mass of dark coats, tall boots, and scarves. I didn't know anyone walking near me, but I told them little good-byes in my head. "I'll never see you again, man in the brown fleece, girl with the bangs. You don't know this, but this may be the last time I walk down Cornmarket Street for a very, very long time." I could smell the Cornish pasties baking at the shop on the corner. I wanted to see and notice everything. A crack in the pavement, a weathered restaurant sign, the hurried feel of getting swept up into pedestrian rush-hour traffic as night set in and people buttoned their coats all the way up.

I cared about the details because when you go somewhere for the first time and you learn so many things there for the first time, you leave, and forever that place, that city, holds so many of your "lessons" that you can't let it go. It's just with you forever, and other people will go to the same city on vacation or a weekend, but they will come back, and the city hasn't grown into a part of them. Plenty of people have gone to Oxford and don't return having grown an imaginary Oxford limb, but so many of us go and do. The place is attached by accident.

The real thing, I guess, is the period of time and what happens in it. Maybe for you it was your first year in high school, or that summer at camp, or the year you had your first job. It's a part of you in a weird, can't-shake-it kind of way, and whatever it is, where we experience the new, deep, and hard things matters and will always matter to us. That's why I paid so much attention to the ground and the streets and the people in Oxford. That's why I went on a walk to say good-bye to a place. Something that could not say good-bye back. Maybe I can't remember your name two minutes after you introduce yourself to me, but Oxford? I remember what it smelled like. I remember how it looked after it rained. Where the homeless people slept. Where the rich people ate and lived. How the buses sounded as they raced past, and how the seats inside them felt after a long day of walking. The pavement's echo under my feet. How the water from the faucet tasted. What my neighbors looked like when they picked up the morning paper.

In the gritty, unique, odd details are the sights, sounds, and smells that changed us. We were someone before we knew and experienced them. We were someone else after.

The sun had not shown itself much that day, and it was dusk now. I had been walking for miles in shoes that weren't made for walking for miles. I stopped at Magdalen Bridge and peered over its edge at the River Cherwell. That part of the river, I knew, would soon meet the Thames. My river. All the roads and paths in Oxford that I wore out and frequented that year seemed to end up at the Thames. It would be the most crooked and winding way, and I would think I was lost, and then there it was, the river, every time. Like the city was a funnel and the Thames its magnetic center.

I clicked through my photographs of the day when I got home. The library, the trees, park benches, bicycles clumped together, their chains tangled in an unsolvable mess. I didn't know I was saying good-bye to more than objects and locations. What wasn't visible to my camera were the parts of me I had left behind, the parts of me I had said good-bye to little by little, layer by layer. The me I had envisioned walking up Headington Hill on Divinity Road for the first time. That me knew things about the world. That me spoke English, knew about God, who God was and how he worked. That me enjoyed shades of black and white, what was right and wrong. That me knew who was wise and who was not. That me had lived inside the church walls, unaware of all these islands off the coasts of nowhere, near the edge of the universe that had so much to offer me. As the day had progressed and I walked all over the city, the north part, the east part, the middle part, I said good-bye to the me I was when I first arrived in Oxford.

Sooner or later we have to say good-bye to that someone we were before. To the parts of us that no longer fit. This is okay, I think. If we continued on in life with every version of us that we have ever been, we would all be very large and heavy people having difficulty walking down the street. Life is about shedding layers, offering up the old skins, like the cricket nymphs do on their brief and painful journeys to adulthood. It is a sacrificial ritual to the earth, this offering of skins.

"Here, earth, are my old skins. They are yours now as I walk forward wearing skin that is a little newer, a little more knowledgeable, or perhaps less knowledgeable, but something more grown up and understanding with wider eyes. Something that is, I hope, more humble and maybe less pretty and taut, but at least more honest."

·⟡·

The night I submitted my thesis, I said good-bye to Jisu for good.

I invited him and some friends, including my new friend Biceps, to celebrate with me at a bar in east Oxford called Kazbar on Cowley Road.

After my river conversation with Jisu, there had been another conversation, at an ice-cream shop. I don't remember the exact words we said, but I remember my ice cream tasted bad in my mouth. At the end, Jisu asked what would be helpful for me going forward, how we should act, and just like that we slid into acquaintance mode. We didn't speak for a while. A superficial text or e-mail here and there, but the tone of us had changed and spending time together no longer made sense.

When Jisu walked into Kazbar, I knew the real reason he had come was not to celebrate my thesis but to say good-bye. He would be leaving for a trip the next day, and I would be off to America before he returned. This was it, our final hour.

He sat on one side of me, and Biceps sat on the other. It was an uncomfortable emotional situation. Feeling joy and relief at finishing my degree while also feeling something deep and sad at the idea of saying good-bye to this person who meant so many things to me.

Jisu leaned over to me. "I have a gift for you," he said in a volume above the noise of the room. He pointed to his bag.

"You do? You didn't have to do that. What is it?"

"I'll give it to you later," he smiled.

Jisu saw someone he knew at a different table and went over to say hi. Biceps sat on my right talking to people, and I was quiet, watching. I told myself I wasn't sad. I tried to match my environment and be happy and celebratory. I didn't want my good-bye with Jisu to be in front of Biceps and everybody, but I didn't want to do it alone either. I didn't want to have more serious conversations and say serious stuff. I didn't want to cry in front of him. I didn't want to apologize. I didn't want him to apologize to me. I wanted to have no feelings about any of it. I wanted a robotic good-bye. A fake semi-good-bye for post-river conversation, post-ice-cream conversation us.

After a while someone finally suggested going somewhere else.

"Yes! Where should we go next?" Biceps asked me.

"Next? Um, I don't know."

Everyone was pulling on coats and moving outside. I stood up with them, and Jisu came along beside me.

"I have to go," he said. "I need to pack for tomorrow."

"Oh yeah, your trip. You can't do one more drink?"

Jisu shook his head and reached into his bag to pull out the gift. It was a book. I read the title, *The Worst-Case Scenario Survival Hand-*

book. It was one of those gift books that illustrates how to survive a stampede of giraffes or how to open a coconut should you find yourself one day on a desert island. I flipped it over and read the back: "Because anything can go wrong, anywhere, at any time."

I smiled and laughed quietly. "Well, I could certainly use this," I said. "Thank you."

"You're welcome."

It was just me and Jisu looking at the book and not at each other for a moment, then everyone was around us, chatting about the weather and who needed to go home and who was staying out. Outside Kazbar with all the people, I couldn't study the book for as long as I wanted to. Jisu and I both knew we didn't have much time. There was no place to talk. He lightly hugged me. We exchanged few words and said less than what was needed.

I think we spend a good portion of our lives saying good-bye. To friends who move and you know, deep down, you will never see again. To men you kissed or never kissed. To cities that are still holding on to a part of your heart. To something you worked toward, dreamed about, told your friends about, and hoped and hoped and hoped for, until hoping no longer brought you joy but pain, and one day you put down the pen with which you wrote that dream and you never return to the page.

There will be many nights when your soul says a reluctant, sad, angry, misunderstood, or baffled good-bye.

And saying good-bye is not a skill you get better at with age. Just watch your mom crying at your grandmother's bedside. Good-byes do not work this way. But for as many dark or sad nights in which you say good-bye, you have the other kind of nights too. Nights when you said hello for the first time to someone who would become a good friend or a central figure in your life. Nights on balconies with wine and the words said over the wine, or maybe because of the wine, that remind you why people say, "Life is rich." You will taste the richness; in that moment, you will taste it and chew on it. The seat beneath you, the glass in front of you, the balcony railing, and the view of the setting sun squeezing between the bars. The clouds above you will spell out promises or possibilities you never thought possible. The people beside you, the grapey aftertaste in your mouth. Your awareness of these things will convince you that what the clouds have spelled out for you is indeed true.

Interspersed with the good-byes, you will have nights of laughter too. Many of those in the backyard with friends you never thought you would meet in a place you never expected to meet them. There will be nights with these friends and new people when the wind feels good and the cold has thawed. Gratitude will slide into your heart and take over, and it will make you laugh even harder.

These nights mixed in with the nights of sad good-byes make the good-byes livable, better, maybe even okay. We live for the wine, the laughter, the balconies, the hellos, and we live with the good-byes.

·ᴄ∽·

A whirlwind of memories spun quickly around me and Jisu as we stood quietly outside Kazbar. I held the book down by my side. Jisu didn't tell me what I had meant to him that year, and I didn't tell him. I stood there reluctant to let the good-bye linger, aware of all the others around us and not knowing how to say good-bye to a best friend, an almost kiss. I looked at the book again. I thought about the weather and how cold it was and how much time in the cold Jisu and I had spent together. How many times we had cycled the very street we stood on now. How we had met up at that coffee shop there and he had listened to me practice my entire presentation on contemporary Irish literature and then helped me pick out a new bike. I thought of the times before the question mark, though it had probably always been there.

I thought about all that, standing outside the bar with friends and strangers still hovering too close. All the memories mashed into one quick one, and I said nothing of them. I did not mention the good times or how Jisu had, on more than one occasion, pulled me out of a dark place in Oxford, pointing me in the direction of light. I didn't tell him how he had been central to my time there, and that I did not want to never see him again. I wanted to say, *See you tomorrow, next week, next month*, anything, but I couldn't. Because there was no promise of seeing each other next week, month, year. So I did the one thing I could. I said the only honest thing I could say. I said good-bye. To my dearest friend, I just said good-bye.

He walked away from me, and I turned back to my friends, back to Biceps, who had been standing there unaware of the tension in the moment. Unaware of the question mark that would follow Jisu home, that would follow me home. Unaware of a friendship that had changed, and had changed me.

14

Tumbleweeds

The tumbleweed came to reside in our garage accidentally—and with every purpose in the world. As a metropolis, Abilene—the city of my undergrad years, the city of infinite crickets—does not have much to offer, but if you've ever wanted to see a real-life tumbleweed cross the road, Abilene is your town.

My roommate's little brother discovered an abnormally large tumbleweed one day while driving his truck down I-20. It was about four feet high and the same wide. He understood a tumbleweed of this size could not be left unappreciated or unseen by everyone he knew. Because it would not fit inside his dorm room, he packed it up in the back of his truck and brought it over to our house. That's how the tumbleweed came to live in our garage.

He was very proud of the tumbleweed, and I grew proud of it as well, though I played no part in discovering it or transporting it. Whenever a visitor came over, I or one of my roommates would inevitably ask, "Wanna see the garage?" And we'd tell the story and enjoy the shocked look on our visitors' faces.

Eventually the novelty of this huge pile of weeds began to wear off, and after a year or so I stopped caring about the tumbleweed as much. I wondered if animals were living in it. It was the ideal environment for birds and squirrels to nest in. I began avoiding the garage for fear of what I might find.

Our tumbleweed burrowed happily and alone in our garage, undisturbed, for a while. But when we graduated and were packing up and moving out, we knew something had to be done with it. We couldn't take it with us. It was too cumbersome. The only solution we could think of was to burn it. It felt wrong to set fire to the thing. Although it had collapsed over time and wasn't the towering figure it once was, our tumbleweed was still a wonder. Killing it would kill its wonder, yet we knew there were no other options.

I wasn't there for the burning. I should have been, but I wasn't. I think my roommate's brother and his friend did it. They rolled it out to our backyard and lit a match. I'm sure it didn't take much time for our enormous, old, dry pile of weeds, sticks, and twigs to become consumed in flame. What took the West Texas winds who knows how long to build took a match no time at all to destroy. The flames rose and with them, bits of tumbleweed, higher and higher until there was nothing left.

I like to think our tumbleweed lives on. That after we killed it with fire, a few twigs remained, and the wind picked them up and rolled them into each other and into other branches and twigs until they formed an equally huge, new-yet-old tumbleweed that rolls across roads in Abilene today. I like to believe a remnant managed to escape the flames. That we aren't able to fully kill anything off, not even with fire. That ashes always rise up and form back together again.

On September 14, 2009, I boarded a bus in Oxford at two o'clock in the morning on St. Clement's Street. The bus would take me to Heathrow so I could board a plane that would fly me back across the Atlantic to where I had come from. I packed my three enormous suitcases and loaded them into a taxi, then out of the taxi and onto the bus. Biceps was there to help me lift them, and Sophie, whose flat was near the bus stop, had woken in the middle of the night to say good-bye.

The three of us stood together in a close triangle in the dead of night, cold, sleepy, and sad. I wondered how I was going to make myself leave them, walk away, and get on a bus. I didn't know how to make my body do that. After a few minutes, the bus driver grew impatient and leaned his head out the door to tell me it was time to go.

Despite how dark it was outside, I could see he had a very large mole on his cheek. Under the pressure of his scowl, I waved good-bye to Sophie and rushed a final kiss to Biceps. Biceps handed me a letter as I stepped on the bus.

I sat in the front row because I wanted to see out all the windows. I wanted to see, as best I could in the night, the city I was leaving. I didn't know if or when I would be back. I wanted to see it as we drove away.

I held the letter in my hand but didn't read it, not yet. As the other passengers slept on the bus, I sat up very alert. I tried to understand what was happening. I had spent a year in a foreign place that spoke my language but didn't. I tried to feel the impact of this and think of memories and replay them as a slide show in my head. I tried to have a very serious and contemplative moment with myself, but I couldn't. Understanding a year's worth of change cannot be forced. So instead, I studied my reflection in the window. I looked the same. Maybe all the clothes I had on were European brands and maybe my hair had grown longer, but overall, still me.

This is how change works. It's stealthy. It delicately changes you and your perspective while you're in it, and it is not until you are fully out of it that you look in the mirror and notice a difference.

I looked through my reflection and out the window. I was not disoriented. I knew the bus was climbing Headington Hill. I knew Brookes was on my left and soon we would pass the grocery store I never went to on my right and that on a nearby corner was a Starbucks where I sometimes went before class. I was well oriented. I had not only lived here, I had settled here, and now, I had to find a way to unsettle. To loosen my grip and face what was in front of me: the road to London, a flight to Texas, and a few days after, a drive to Nashville.

After looking out the window for a while, I decided to open Biceps's letter. With sporadic streetlamps as my only lighting, I read it. One. Staccato. Sentence. At a time. He said kind things. He said he was glad he had decided to move back to the States, so we wouldn't be far from each other. He said that when he thinks back on the last few weeks, his and my final weeks in Oxford, he sees me and us as a picture hanging above his mantel, a figure central to his life at the time.

I thought that was such a lovely description. I still do. We all have people over our mantels, don't we? The frames and the faces change as we go along, but we remember each of them. They have imprinted us in one way or another. All the people who make up so much of who we are and are becoming. No matter how far from them we go, no matter how disparate our twigs and sticks and leaves are in the end, the people over our mantels have played a part in creating us, and that keeps them with us in a way that no fire can burn up. The ashes are not too dry to be brought back to life, and what is created from them is always better than what was before.

A lot changes and scatters in young adulthood. Your surroundings, your circumstances, your friends, your beliefs, and yourself. We are, don't forget, at our core, like baby cricket nymphs. The creatures that shed skin in order to grow. The small bugs that make sacrifices to the earth as they become older. The layers fall away slowly, one at a time, and we morph into something else, and rarely do things turn out the way we think they will, and rarely do we end up looking the way we think we will look.

After an experience like my intense year in Oxford, you sort of think you're done. You've morphed into what you will be. You know what you believe in and what you don't. It's been tested. The worst and the best—it has all happened. You've learned what you came to learn in life and the rest of your days will be spent living what you've learned and coasting on that knowledge. Nothing will compare. Nothing will be as rich as that, or as full or as hard or as sad. This is what we tell ourselves in order to enter the next phase.

After I left Oxford though, life and learning didn't stop. Our individual journeys are ongoing. They are not a yearlong trip overseas. More has happened. So many events and things to make me see that the person on the bus on the way to Heathrow actually understood very little. I sit here, nearly twenty-nine years old, and I feel more unraveled than I did at twenty-two, wandering the lonely, old streets of Oxford town. I am not who I will always be. I don't know much at all. I have seen only a tiny pocket of the world and met only a tiny fraction of God's people. The things written in this book are from one year. One year. That is not even a gasp of a breath on the scale of knowledge in the kingdom of God.

That's what this collection of stories is, I guess. Not a few pages about how to live, but a few pages reminding us that youth and its feelings of uncertainty, constant change, and insecurity are the perpetual way of the Christian life. Learning never ends. Change is continuous. The questions never stop. I'm not sure if that sounds hopeful, but it's meant to. Our faith, how we feel about it and how we feel about God, was never meant to be static. We should never assume we have "arrived." Because the moment we do, something happens that we didn't expect or don't understand, and we are flattened by the reality of our lack of knowledge once again.

I brought it home with me when I left Oxford. That old, muddy trail by the River Thames. It stayed close by. I return to it again and again still. Sometimes just at the last minute, when I don't know what else to do. When life feels uncomfortably jerked between nights of hellos and nights of good-byes, I stare at my little Thames and say to God with shoulders shrugged, "I am at a loss here." I look for the ripples over the stones to form some sort of message for me. Some sort of sign that will tell me what to do next. I want a fortune-telling river. But this is not what rivers are for, I've learned. They are not here to tell us our fortunes or to answer all our what, when, where, and why questions. Rivers are here to simply be here.

So my hope is changing. As the river ripples by and as I plod along, I hope we have long, rambling, never-ending conversations about all the things I need to talk about and all the things he needs to tell me. A river conversation in which not much of anything is resolved but a relationship of trust and assurance is formed, and I walk the muddy trail until I am very, very old, and the river, it flows and flows and flows.

A few weeks before the bus ride to Heathrow, there was this little moment I remember in a café on the second floor of my favorite bookshop in Oxford. A small moment, a mere second, really, when I sat across from a friend at a table by the window that gave us a view of the ancient school's library and a cobblestone alley below. My plane ticket home was purchased. I knew I was headed elsewhere. But this day, on an uncharacteristically hot afternoon, I did not think of the future. I was, uncharacteristically, present, and I thought about my location, right then. Even though I had been in Oxford a year, I could not believe I was here. I could not believe I was sitting across from someone I had come to know and who had come to know me, all the way across an ocean in this other country, in this other place. The thought made me feel small and made God feel very big. Like when Lucy is talking to Aslan:

"Aslan," said Lucy, "you're bigger."
"That is because you are older, little one," answered he.

"Not because you are?"

"I am not. But every year you grow, you will find
me bigger."[11]

In the second-story café, at the table in the corner, the sun melted through the window's glass. It cast part of my arm in shadow and part of it in light, and in the coldest town I have ever known, I felt honestly warm.

---

11. C. S. Lewis, *Prince Caspian* (New York: HarperCollins, 1951), 141.

Acknowledgments

How do I begin here except to say this book would not exist without the people I'm about to address? They are much more than the "acknowledged" or the "thanked." They are the ones who pushed this along when I wanted to quit, who told me where to turn next when the path had grown dark, and whose mere presence gave me the courage to say what I felt I needed to say. This book is not mine. It's ours.

To the friends I've written about: Thank you for letting me share a part of your story. You've taught me more than you know.

To Oxford: Is it strange to thank a city? Oh well. I'm going to anyway. Thank you for giving me space to wander.

To the WaterBrook team: It is a miracle every time a book gets out the door, and you are the miracle workers.

To my editor, John Blase: At this point, these words are just as much yours as they are mine and all I know to say is, thank you.

To Karen Hill: Your suggestions for this book were invaluable. You've nudged me toward writing ever since I can remember. I will always be so grateful.

To Steve Green: You are so much more than an agent. You are a dear and trusted friend, and if there was a second dedication page, you would be on it.

To Nashville friends, like Kathie and Erica and so many others: Thank you for cheering me on, even when I was on the floor in tears over this thing. You have no idea how your encouragement has carried me.

To Jenna and Sara: The only reason you didn't show up more on these pages is because we were an ocean apart when all this stuff happened. To have sisters who are also best friends is no small gift. Trust me, you are on every page.

To my mom and dad: You've read this book as many times as I have by now. Your support, love, and care are everything to me. How fitting it is to begin and end this book acknowledging you. I love you.